The Achievement of Walter Scott

by the same author
ANTHONY TROLLOPE
ANGLICAN ATTITUDES
THE IMAGINATION OF CHARLES DICKENS
THE UNBELIEVERS

The Achievement of
Walter Scott

A. O. J. COCKSHUT

NEW YORK UNIVERSITY PRESS
1969

First published 1969
First U.S. edition 1969

Second Printing, March, 1971

Contents

Preface

PART ONE *THE LITERARY PERSONALITY*

    1 *Sketch of a Career*   11

    2 *The Two Voices*   30

    3 *The Prophetic and the Social*   42

    4 *Cause and Effect*   63

    5 *Mediaevalist and Entertainer*   90

PART TWO *THE MAJOR NOVELS*

    1 *Waverley*   107

    2 *Old Mortality*   129

    3 *Rob Roy*   152

    4 *The Heart of Midlothian*   171

    5 *Redgauntlet*   193

The author's Edition of *The Waverley Novels*. Adam & Charles Black. Edinburgh 1871.
The Letters of Sir Walter Scott. Centenary Edition edited by H. J. C. Grierson: Constable 1932.
The Prose Works of Sir Walter Scott, Bart. 28 vols: Edinburgh 1834.
The Journal of Sir Walter Scott 1825-1832. New Edition, Edinburgh 1910.

Preface

This book is written out of three simple convictions. I am convinced that Scott wrote a number of books which deserve to have an enduring classic status. I am convinced that to see this it is necessary to discriminate very sharply. Few, if any, of our greatest authors wrote such a mass of careless and inferior work. Moreover, the lines of division, in the main, are strikingly clear. The second half of this volume discusses in detail the five books which form the core of achievement. To these can be added without reservation *The Two Drovers* and *The Highland Widow*, and, with various exceptions and allowances, *The Bride of Lammermoor* and *A Legend of Montrose*. In addition, there are two books which are masterly in part, but contain inferior or discordant elements—*Guy Mannering* and *The Antiquary*. Of the rest of Scott's voluminous writings, much is sensible, superficial stuff, written by a busy, intelligent, man of the world in the spirit of a journalist, much was exciting at the time it was written but can never, so far as we can see, be so again, and some is downright sensational and trashy.

The third conviction is that we understand Scott best by concentrating on his strength and passing lightly over his weakness. His is not a case, like Byron, where the whole flawed, strange personality seems to be equally present in his best and his worst performances. It is rather a case where the central core of genius is either mysteriously present and functioning or it is not. When it is not, there is no use at all in seeking for it, and only a humble kind of historical use in analysing what is then produced. It has been my assumption that Scott's greatness lies in his achievement as a novelist. I have used the letters, the literary criticism and the story of his life, but sparingly, and only when they seemed to help the understanding of the fiction. I have passed lightly over the antiquarian Scott and ignored the poet altogether.

Even when the subject is thus limited, Scott has several different kinds of appeal. One in particular seems to me to matter most. Scott took the concept of society current in the works of the great eighteenth century writers, whether novelists, poets or historians, and showed that it was radically inadequate. It was inadequate because society could *change* and each person must react to this. The best way to show this was to show a society in the process of becoming something different while confronting an alien tradition in military or political conflict. Here is the germ of the justification of the historical novel as a serious form. If this is your true subject you cannot show it without a long perspective. The essential point about Scott, which has often been forgotten and usually been ignored, was made by Leslie Stephen, when he said: "Scott understood and nobody has better illustrated by example, the true mode of connecting past and present."[1] This book is an extended comment on that proposition.

[1] Leslie Stephen: *Hours in a Library*, New Ed 1892 vol I p159. The whole essay is of interest.

PART ONE

The Literary Personality

1 *Sketch of a Career*

The history of Scott's life day by day is known in immense detail, and even a summary of this vast quantity of material would be out of place here. This chapter attempts two things, to give a sketch of a very complex literary personality, and to trace the line of achievement and decline discernible in the novels.

Down to 1814, his forty-third year, Scott was, whether knowingly or not, preparing himself for his years of achievement. From 1814 to 1819 he produced work of merit and originality surpassed by few and of quantity equalled by none of our leading writers of any century. In the course of this extraordinary achievement, which was further cumbered by a more than ordinary share of the duties of a working man of the world, he destroyed his health for ever. From 1819 till shortly before his death in 1832 he continued to work very hard, and produced many books almost all of which have some merit. But with one very notable exception, *Redgauntlet*, they are all affected in varying degrees by haste, fatigue, ill-health, and the consequent vices of clumsiness, repetition and strained sensationalism.

Between 1820 and 1825 this man of great intellectual powers and of superhuman energies was coming gradually to realize that he was overworking, and that both his own health and the rich imaginative sources of his work were becoming exhausted. In 1824 he was able to collect himself, and, by taking a long backward look at his own youth and at the final consequences of the Jacobite rebellion about which he had thought and written so much, to write *Redgauntlet*. It would have been possible for an early reader of *Redgauntlet* to make several different guesses about what might have followed. Scott might have moved to a serene, relaxed old age, or to a more fundamental renewal of inspiration, or to the harmless magnificence of the grand old man. But none of these things came to pass. Instead, the financial collapse of 1825 and the ensuing burden of debt caused a continuation and strengthening of the trends of the previous five or six years. From then on he literally wrote himself to death.

In its general pattern—preparation, achievement, decline—Scott's career is usual enough. But very unusual and, so far as I know, unique are the proportions within the pattern. The period of preparation is extraordinarily long as well as being very fully used. From boyhood until he was over forty Scott was avidly searching for the visible relics of history and for its literary remains. He brooded long hours and long years about certain grand historical themes, the Jacobite rebellions, the Scottish Reformation, the struggles of the Covenanters against the Stuart kings. All this time he was a hard-working and effective man of the world and a rising literary man. His poetry, to which he himself attached little importance, was enough to make him one of the most famous men of the day. But the deepest powers of his mind were as yet unused. He was picking his way through life with the safe judgment of a sleepwalker. He was not, so far as we can tell, consciously waiting or consciously preparing himself; at the deepest level he was reticent, and he gives no sign of persistent curiosity about the sources of his inspiration. In no respect is the contrast with his great contemporaries, Wordsworth and Coleridge, more complete.

In 1814, suddenly, the barriers were down. In five weeks, while carrying out his ordinary duties as Writer to the Signet, and all the engagements of a busy man, he wrote a long,

12

extraordinarily original and immensely distinguished novel
—*Waverley.*[1] It remains almost, if not quite, his greatest
achievement. Between 1815 and 1818, while remaining a
busy man in many ordinary ways, and in addition to many
writings of less importance, he published *Guy Mannering, The
Antiquary, Rob Roy, The Black Dwarf, Old Mortality,* and *The
Heart of Midlothian.* In 1819 he was writing *Ivanhoe,* perhaps
the first of his works to show that fatal facility and neglect of
the sources of his serious inspiration which affected so many
later books. But he also published two works of considerable
merit, *The Bride of Lammermoor* and *A Legend of Montrose.* But
The Bride was dictated while he was suffering acute physical
pain, and the ensuing breakdown in health was serious and
prolonged.

The works that follow, *The Monastery, Kenilworth, The
Fortunes of Nigel,* and four or five others have various merits,
and are all quite obviously the writings of an exceptional
man. *The Pirate* may be singled out for its originality, and
St Ronan's Well for its honest attempt to achieve something
alien to the author's temperament, the comedy of Jane
Austen. Yet in none of these books can we feel that the
author's talents are being used to the full. In each difficulties
are avoided; and intrigues are unravelled with what can
only be called effrontery.

But there is one incident in Scott's life during these years
of continuing fame and fortune and real literary decline on
which I want to focus some attention. It is the visit of George
IV to Edinburgh in 1822, the year after his coronation. Before the King's accession the two men were fairly well-
acquainted. George as Prince Regent had entertained Scott
at what he called 'snug little dinners'[2], and unlike all his

---

[1] He had written a few early chapters some years before, but
these are a small proportion of the whole.
[2] *Lockhart* vol v, 46.

predecessors since Charles II, and unlike his successors, George was a man who could talk sensibly about artistic matters. His admiration for Scott was genuine.

And yet, Scott approached the court with hesitation. On 6 November 1813 he had written in a letter to Byron: "I am somewhat an admirer of royalty, and in order to maintain this part of my creed, I shall take care never to be connected with a court, but stick to the *ignotum pro mirabili*."[1] But this determination was weakened by his attendance at the coronation in 1821. This ceremony appealed strongly to his feeling for tradition and pageantry, and, being the first for sixty years, it had the charm of novelty as well. Scott began to wonder if he was destined to be the reconciler of the Hanoverians to the Scottish people. As soon as this idea occurred, Scott must have seemed to himself and others the ideal person for the task. He was a loyal subject of the crown, yet a lover of Jacobite antiquities, and a sound Anglican who understood the heart of the Lowland Covenanters. He was even the chronicler of the Porteous riots, the most serious episode of Scottish unrest in the time of the new King's ancestor, George II.

But if Scott had unique qualifications for the task, he was also in the grip of internal contradictions. Lockhart records, on the King's first arrival by sea: "his Majesty called for a bottle of Highland whisky, and having drunk his [Scott's] health in this national liquor, desired a glass to be filled for him. Sir Walter, after draining his own bumper, made a request that the King would condescend to bestow on him the glass out of which his Majesty had just drunk his health; and this being granted, the precious vessel was immediately wrapped up and carefully deposited in what he conceived to be the safest part of his dress."[2] Now, granted that Scott was honestly convinced of the value of hereditary monarchy,

[1] *Letters* vol III p373.   [2] *Lockhart* VII 53-4.

granted that he thought it was his serious duty to help to end traditional Scottish hatreds by focussing loyalty on the now long-established Hanoverian line, it is hard to avoid seeing an element either of play-acting or of solemn absurdity in this scene. Lockhart, an uneven writer who could be over-solemn himself (as well as what Scott never was, untruthful), is at his best here. He sees that what was really happening was a kind of re-enactment of the Edinburgh scenes of *Waverley*, with the gross, self-pitying and debauched king of sixty substituted for the young, fearless (and not yet de-bauched) Prince Charlie, "with the Great Unknown[1] him-self for his Baron Bradwardine, *ad exuendas vel detrahendas caligas domini regis post battalium.*"[2] There was nothing in the least accidental about the parallel. The whole emphasis of the celebrations, in which Scott played Master of Cere-monies, was on the Highlands, the primitive source of Jaco-bite power. The King did what no respectable citizen of Edinburgh at that time would have thought of doing, he wore Highland tartan.

Are we to call all this magnificent or absurd? Was it a far-sighted, statesmanlike (and very effective) reconciliation of the ancient antagonisms of Scotland, and was the play-acting a legitimate appeal for a serious and humane purpose to the imagination of the public? Or was Scott with the King's help the founder of the bogus tradition of Scotsman-ship that can be studied in the advertising pages of expensive American magazines? Perhaps the answer is 'both,' and, if so, then the ambiguity corresponds to the ambiguity in Scott's own mind. He was fond of describing himself as 'an incorrigible Jacobite,'[3] and felt sure that he would have

[1] i.e. Scott, not yet publicly known to be the author of the *Waverley* novels.
[2] *Lockhart* VII 50 cf. *Waverley* chap 14.
[3] e.g. *Letters* vol IX p335, dated 29 Dec 1825.

taken arms for the Pretender if he had lived in his time. Yet he was not only a loyal subject of the Georges; he was convinced at a deep level of the necessity and rightness of England's decision to cast off the Stuarts. And he saw the matter, of course, with his powerful historical intelligence, in all its bearings, not just as a choice between dynasties, but as involving every important question of political and cultural development. His deepest meditations on these themes are embodied in *Waverley, Rob Roy* and *Redgauntlet*. But perhaps *Rob Roy* comes nearest to giving his sober, waking vision of the whole matter. The daylight judgment is strikingly, even bitterly, opposed to the Stuart cause.

Nor is this the only ambiguity. Granted, as any sensible man had to grant in 1822, that the Hanoverian kings were firmly established and the cause of civil peace lay in supporting them, there was an ambiguity in his whole attitude to the throne and the person of the King. Scott, on the whole, liked people, but took a low view of their virtues and capacities. He did not carry his enthusiasm so far as to be dazzled by George IV. Not only did he draw a distinction between the office and the person of the monarch, as all sensible monarchists must do, he was even violent in his assertion of civic rights against the King. For instance, it was suggested that, in view of the quarrel between George IV and his son-in-law Prince Leopold, the inscription in honour of the latter should be removed from a place where the King would see it. Scott said: "Sooner than that inscription should be erased, or even covered with flags and flowers . . . I would with my own hands set the town of Edinburgh on fire, and destroy it."[1]

It is extraordinarily difficult, then, to give a balanced assessment of Scott's most influential and spectacular moment in public life. The far-seeing man of good will, the play-

---

[1] As reported by Captain Hall cf. *Lockhart* VII p291.

actor, the romantic antiquary, the experienced man of the world who takes things as they come—all these are present. But one feature in particular should be noticed, and it is easy to miss it. Scott's great political success here was achieved by a bold, even reckless stroke. To reconcile the Lowlands to England and its dynasty by an extravagant glorification of the Highlands, chief seat of opposition to that dynasty, was a most dangerous course. For Scott on this occasion, as sometimes, though not always, in his writings, effrontery paid. It is easy to forget this because Scott was at the same time such an easy-going, well-rooted, enjoying man.

But the crash of 1825 revealed sterner qualities. Out of the complicated history of Scott's financial affairs, two points are relevant here. Scott was, in fact, though not in intention, a most reckless spender. Here, too, the psychological causes are complex. In all that appealed to the senses, he was a lover of coarse and plentiful simplicity. But he had a peculiar kind of materialistic imaginativeness that was in practice much more damaging to his prospects than any ordinary extravagance could have been. His mind moved, wildly but not altogether selfishly, through images of great towers, of wildernesses become fertile land, of forests, of generously treated and contented peasants. His hospitality combined in an unusual way the magnificent with the homely and personal. As Virginia Woolf saw,[1] the episode of the gas was deeply characteristic. He loved a bright light, because it appealed to the imagination and stimulated gaiety; he was oblivious of the immense expense, trouble and waste of installing gas in a private house at that time.

The other main characteristic, which made any financial recovery impossible and turned his last years into a time of drudgery, was the delicate sense of honour which made it

[1] 'Gas at Abbotsford' in *The Moment* 1947.

impossible for him to blame anyone but himself for a joint misfortune, and made the thought of unpaid creditors intolerable. So from 1825 to 1832 we have the sad picture of a man earning immense sums of money, which were always far too much for the good of his art and too little to achieve solvency. The journal which he kept in his last years is full of phrases like: 'My poverty but not my will consents.'

From 1814 to 1827 the authorship of the *Waverley* novels was theoretically secret. Some people knew and many guessed that Scott was the author, but there was always enough mystery and speculation to keep public interest in the question alive. At a theatrical dinner on 23 February 1827, Lord Meadowbank, after asking Scott's permission, revealed the secret in his speech, and Scott rose to reply for the first time as the admitted author of the *Waverley* novels. A few months later, in the Introduction to *Chronicles of the Canongate*, he wrote the fullest account he ever gave of his process of composition. It is in some respects still a superficial account; it does not attempt to analyse the deeper sources of inspiration. But it shows several things clearly. First, in its discussion of the sources of *Waverley* it shows the paramount importance of oral tradition. Learned, intelligent and bookish though Scott always was, there is something lacking in his novels when oral tradition is absent. Then this introduction brings out very well one of the central paradoxes, which can be seen equally in his literary and in his financial affairs. He was at the same time over-ambitious and over-modest. When he writes: "When I made the discovery—for to me it was one—that by amusing myself with composition, which I felt a delightful occupation, I could also give pleasure to others, and became aware that literary pursuits were likely to engage in future a considerable portion of my time . . ." the casual anti-artistic tone is no affectation. Yet he writes generally, both in his masterpieces and in his potboilers, as if he could do anything, as if he were the king

18

of literature to whom no law applied, and whom no consideration of common sense could touch. Similarly, he shows at the same time a disdain for literary fame coupled with an intense pride in it. As he wrote in his journal only a little after writing this introduction (12 Dec 1827): 'They cannot say but what I had the crown.'

Much earlier, in the Quarterly Review of 1817, he had written a more detailed piece of self-criticism. It has to be handled with caution because it was, from one point of view, part of the great spoof-game about the authorship of the novels that Scott and some of his intimates played with such zest right up to 1827. Scott took care to write in a way that seems unnatural in a man writing about himself. But if we keep this difficulty in mind, we can still learn something of his attitude to his own work from the article. The first impression we have is that Scott's judgment of himself is extraordinarily detached. True, he was acting the part of detachment; but he could not possibly have played it so well if he had had the sense of personal identification with his work which was so characteristic of his great contemporaries, especially Blake and Wordsworth. Thus he says of *The Black Dwarf*: "Neither hero nor heroine excites interest of any sort, being just the sort of *pattern* people whom nobody cares a farthing about."[1] Yet there are moments when his genuine modesty is overcome by the pride of creation, or perhaps we should say, by detached admiration as if the work had been done by another. His praise of Meg Merrilies is especially revealing of the multiple mind of the author: "The Scottish peasant speaks the language of his native country, his *national* language, not the *patois* of an individual district; and in listening to it we not only do not experience even the slightest feeling of disgust or aversion, but our bosoms are responsive to every sentiment of sublimity, or awe, or terror,

[1] *Prose Works*, XIX, 27.

which the author may be disposed to excite. Of the truth of all this Meg Merrilies is a sufficiently decisive instance. The terrible graces of this mysterious personage, an outcast and profligate of the lowest class, are complete in their effect, though conveyed by the *medium* of language that has hitherto been connected with associations that must have altogether neutralized them."[1]

This passage is very near the heart of Scott's mystery, and merits close attention. The first thing we notice is that the critical terms are entirely traditional. It would not be precisely true to say that Scott is preaching a revolutionary critical doctrine by means of Augustan language. For the point is that it is not only the words but the basic assumptions that are Augustan. The idea that the common speech of the Scottish peasant is unsuitable for tragic or sublime effects is first sincerely accepted, and then disposed of as if by magic. In some undefined way, Meg Merrilies and similar figures in the novels are exceptions. As literary criticism this is incurious and perfunctory. But it would really be a mistake to regard it as literary criticism at all. The real point lies in the tension between 'terrible graces' and 'profligate of the lowest class'. The first phrase is a paradox that stands out boldly from the slightly tired Augustan prose; the second is the unimpeachable but inadequate judgment of the sensible man of the world.

But what are we to make of the incuriosity of a man who could present this contradiction and leave it with reconciliation not even attempted? Haste partly, distaste for 'useless' abstract questions, partly, but most of all, I think a kind of fear. He felt the glory and the strangeness in the depths of his own work. How could he help it? But he would not allow his strange vision to rule his life. Not only was he a respected Edinburgh professional man. He was also a sensible Augustan

[1] *ibid* 67.

intellectual and a judicious admirer of Dryden. And so, he writes of the Covenanters in the true tradition of Hume and Robertson: "A party so wild in their principles, so vague and inconsistent in their views, could not subsist long under a free and unlimited toleration."[1] He meant it, but anyone who reads *Old Mortality* will refuse to believe it.

Occasionally, the conflict of literary principles in his own mind became so obvious that it embarrassed him. Then he would escape by clowning and comic self-depreciation. Thus he ends his introduction to *The Two Drovers*, one of his most impressive delineations of tragic emotions in humble life, with the ridiculous words: "An oyster may be crossed in love, says the gentle Tilburina—and a drover may be touched on a point of honour, says the Chronicler of the Canongate." Nothing could be better calculated to make the reader expect something quite different from what he is going to get; but at least a veil of humour is drawn over the tattered standard of Augustan theory.

I spoke just now of fear, but I did not mean timidity and tepid conformism. I meant rather a religious awe, to which he could not wholly yield. He could not yield to it because there were other equally genuine sides of his nature to which he must also be true. He was above all a multiple personality. He would not have been the great writer he was if he had allowed the prosy antiquary, or the visionary democrat or the Augustan gentleman or the Edinburgh lawyer to dominate. The lover of the extraordinary, the constructor of wildly improbable plots, was also the sensible man who painted the humdrum in glowing colours: "Jeanie's fancy, though not the most powerful of her faculties, was lively enough to transport her to a wild farm in Northumberland, well-stocked with milk-cows, yeald beasts, and sheep; a meeting-house hard by, frequented by serious Presbyterians, who had

[1] *ibid* 84.

united in a harmonious call to Reuben Butler to be their spiritual guide;—Effie restored, not to gaiety but to cheerfulness at least;—their father with grey hairs smoothed down, and spectacles on his nose; herself, with the maiden snood exchanged for a matron's curch—all arranged in a pew in the said meeting-house, listening to words of devotion, rendered sweeter and more powerful by the affectionate ties which combined them with the preacher."[1]

A good deal of what he would have called his prosiness, and what later readers have called his dullness, can be explained, though not excused, by the tensions of this multiple personality. All his imaginary editors and writers of introductions are bores. In part, this is the likable though tedious self-depreciation of the sensible man of the world, who knows that his antiquarian enthusiasms are mildly eccentric. But more than that, these characters are a device to separate out the faculties of his mind. Without the antiquary in him, his best novels could not have been written, and it is the antiquary in him in part that accounts for his obvious unlikeness to most of his peers in the art of fiction.

But he knew, too, that antiquarianism could drown his art if its full flood was permitted to engulf his stories. The effect of the imaginary narrators is to give a frame. The Edinburgh lawyer and the Augustan gentleman never allowed the visionary to have it all his own way even for a time. Sometimes there is a startling disproportion between an event as described and the author's comment upon it which follows immediately. Thus in *The Pirate* evocations of the romantic north, and the dooms and prophecies of a dying civilization alternate with intelligent, Johnsonian accounts of the relation of agricultural methods to the state of social classes. It is characteristic of Scott, though it would be alien to almost any other author, to make Halcro, the

[1] *Heart of Midlothian* chap 39.

wild northern bard, when we expect him to come out with desperate tales of ancient Nordic revenge, to come out as a devoted admirer of—John Dryden.

The Pirate is set in the Orkneys and Shetlands, a part of the world where Scott was only a moderately well-informed occasional visitor. He was fascinated by but not deeply versed in the Nordic past of the islands. The plot he invents for the occasion, like many of the plots of his less distinguished novels, is melodramatic enough. But Scott avoids as completely as Johnson[1] does the fundamental error of romantic distance. He never forgets that what is strange to visitors and students from a different culture is not strange to the inhabitants. Thus he writes: 'To a stranger these evident marks and tokens of human misery might, at the first glance, form a contrast with the scene of mirth with which they were now associated; but the association was so familiar to the natives that it did not for a moment interrupt the course of their glee.''[2]

Everywhere in Scott's life and personality extremes meet. The following story, narrated by Captain Hall,[3] is typical of one side of his nature: "In the course of a conversation about ghosts, fears in the dark, and such matters, Sir Walter mentioned having once arrived at a country inn, when he was told there was no bed for him. 'No place to lie down at all? said he. 'No', said the people of the house—'none, except a room in which there is a corpse lying.' 'Well', said he, 'did the person die of any contagious disorder?' 'Oh no—not at all', said they. 'Well, then,' continued he, 'let me have the other bed.—So' said Sir Walter, 'I laid me down, and never had a better night's sleep in my life.' " This is the same man who had an abiding interest in ghosts and praeternatural horrors. Perhaps, however, the latter should not be taken

---

[1] *A Journey to the Western Islands of Scotland,* 1775.
[2] *The Pirate* chap 12.   [3] cf. *Lockhart* VII, 298.

too seriously, being more of an intellectual hobby than a deep trait of personality. But at any rate there can be no doubt that he was deeply emotional and impressionable; he was not trifling when he said that if he did not see the heather each year he should die.

There is a paradox, too, in his method of writing. Few, if any, great writers ever wrote so fast as Scott and with such apparent ease. He always seemed to his guests to have all day to spare, to be the least busy of men, because he wrote mainly in the hours before breakfast. The sentences formed themselves spontaneously in his mind, and he was never at a loss for a word or a paragraph or a chapter. This contrasts not only with the content of the books but with the effect of authorship upon him.

It is not just that his best books are so good. They are also full of tension. No doubt the melodramatic and violent events came easily enough. But how can anyone write *easily* in the deeply serious vein of *Waverley* and *Old Mortality* about the conflict of civilizations? Perhaps the answer is that he did not, that the ease was only an appearance, though the rapidity, certainly, was genuine enough. Like a great athlete, Scott had the power to spend himself completely in a maximum effort, which appears effortless to the onlookers. But he did not, like an athlete, rest and recover for the next great effort. Hence exhaustion and much inferior work; and, unlike the athlete again, he lacked the power to distinguish his best work from the rest.

The relation between general cultural conditions and the formation of the mind of the great writer is always obscure. But without venturing to speak in terms of cause and effect, we can say that there are points of close similarity between the mind of Scott and the late eighteenth century Edinburgh élite among which he grew up. Hume died when Scott was a child, in 1776, and in the following year Robertson published his *History of America*. Henry Mackenzie was twenty-six years older than Scott, and Burns twelve years older. These four great names, together with all that they represent of less eminent but still talented men, are an indication of a strangely divided literary culture. Hume, one of the most acute minds of the eighteenth century in any country, can be called, if you like, Augustan. The assumptions that he makes in his history about monarchy, and about the Constitution, his dismissal of Cromwell as a 'hypocritical fanatic' —these are impeccably Augustan. Yet in the deeper qualities of mind and heart which the highest achievements in literature (Augustan and other kinds) require imperatively, Hume is obviously deficient. So in a less marked degree is Robertson. Henry Mackenzie might be thought to have redressed the balance. He isolated and developed what Hume ignored or despised, the vein of sentiment and curious emotion. But the fundamental difference between English and Scots literature in the years 1740-1790 may be expressed in epigrammatic form by saying that Dr. Johnson lived in London. That is to say, in England a late Augustan synthesis was possible. Humane, deeply emotional, and thoroughly Augustan, Johnson could accept, admire and use both Dryden and Richardson. He could respond, as strongly as Gray, but with a much more penetrating mind than Gray, to Celtic antiquities. While maintaining the validity of Augustan generality, and following its spirit in his own poetry and his literary criticism, he could become the first biographer of the modern type. He could become this because he assumed that every casual detail of daily life and every quirk of personality was significant. But, I repeat, the Johnsonian synthesis, far-reaching though it is, is still indisputably Augustan. Among all the unlikely candidates proposed since Arnold's time for the onerous office of 'herald of the romantic dawn', Johnson at least has been omitted.

Why is it that we feel at once, that a Scots Dr. Johnson, if the momentary invention of such a monster may be forgiven, could not have synthesised Hume and Mackenzie? Edwin Muir,[1] in a fascinating and perhaps extreme analysis, accounted for it as an inevitable consequence of the linguistic situation in Scotland. The Scots language was dying, but was still sufficiently alive to prevent any Scotsman from using English like a native. One language for thought, study and serious literature, and another for conversation must lead, Muir thought, to the maimed Augustanism of a great man like Hume, and to the petty, lifeless Augustanism of all the forgotten genteel versifiers of Edinburgh. But, of course, the late eighteenth century Scots poet, who is remembered to-day, was not like that at all. The man who is remembered is Burns, and the key case in Muir's indictment is the case of Burns; and here a Londoner like me must tread more carefully than a native of the Orkneys. But Muir's case against Burns is hard to answer, though it can, no doubt, be simply dismissed. It is that, in his love poetry especially, feeling is treated as an absolute; and that Burns, a man obviously of high natural intelligence, cannot use his intelligence and his feelings at the same time. And Muir has some impressive examples from Scottish poetry of earlier centuries to show that it was not always so, and that men, perhaps of less natural endowment than Burns had in the past been able to bring the intellect and feelings into play simultaneously just as English poets had done.

It may be that Muir's condemnations are too sweeping, but he is surely right in seeing the key to the whole question in the relation between the English and Scots language. Scott, with characteristic boldness, attempts to cut the knot by using both English and Scots in the same book, and often on the same page. Now the generally accepted judgment about this is embodied in the words of Virginia Woolf: describing Scott's English conversation with his friends, inter-

[1] Edwin Muir: *Scott and Scotland*, 1936.
26

spersed with Scottish ballads and fragments, she says: 'So it happens, too, in the novels—the lifeless English gives way to the living Scots."[1] It is this judgment that I wish to dispute.

Now, clearly, like all generally accepted judgments, it has a good deal of rough fidelity to fact. Scott uses the Scots language in the novels exclusively for dialogue. He was a great master of dialogue, and a selection of his most memorable passages would probably include a great preponderance of dialogue. Moreover, and this is a more telling point, his Scots dialogue is more impressive and memorable than his English dialogue. Here Muir's analysis, that a Scotsman born in the eighteenth century tended to use English for thought and Scots for feeling seems to work admirably. "The pattern people whom nobody cares a farthing about" generally speak in English. The tough peasants, the humorous servants, the visionary outcasts like Meg Merrilies, speak in Scots. It seems that Virginia Woolf has a very good case.

But she is wrong, in my view, because she is trying to reduce what is valuable in Scott to one side of this multiple personality. She forgets that the wild utterances of Meg Merrilies or Madge Wildfire would have little value if they were a simple expression of the author's emotions. The greatness of Scott does not lie in his lyric poetry but in his novels. And a novelist, if he is not to end by belittling life and boring the reader must allow for many different types of feeling. He must not only show but judge. In his greatest works Scott does this. He shows the feeling of the diehard Jacobite remnant (who, incidentally do not always speak in Scots) or the covenanting peasants, or the mad gypsy in an intelligible pattern, within an intelligible frame. To say that the lifeless English gives way to the living Scots, plausible as it is, is in the end as uncritical and short-sighted as to make

[1] V. Woolf. Op. cit. p53.

a selection of the beauties of Shakespeare. The play's the thing; and the novel's the thing. In his best works I believe (and here I differ somewhat from Muir) Scott turned to artistic gain the disastrous division of Scots culture and language into 'rational English' and 'feeling Scots.'

We have seen plainly enough in this chapter that Scott was a man driven by many contradictory impulses. But it would go against our general sense of his nature to call him a divided man. If we agree that that is a phrase which fits his friend Byron, it will become obvious that it does not fit Scott. In Scott's personality, as those who knew him best understood it, in his finest writings as we know them, there were harmonizing forces stronger than the contradictions. The contrast with Byron is clear. Scott was genial, kindly, modest in life, where Byron was rude, reckless, unpredictable. Scott was attached to his native soil where Byron was a restless wanderer. And so in their writings. Above all Scott is kind, balanced, fair. How with the divided literary heritage described by Muir, and with the powerful incongruities we have seen within his own nature could he achieve this? He achieved it by coolly examining all the outer and inner divisions, instead of, like Byron, merely allowing them to torture him within, and emerge in the violent transitions and palpable disharmonies of his work. In fact, Byron experienced conflict, and allowed it to distort his poetry. Scott thought and wrote about conflict, especially the conflict of whole nations, whole cultures, whole classes, whole religious and political traditions. He could not have done this so well, he could not have brought the intelligent academic mind and the feeling heart to bear *together*, without making use of the existing division between the educated Edinburgh English of Hume, and the rough Lowland Scots of Burns. 'Lifeless English and living Scots' is a false opposition because it overlooks the fact that for Scott the analytical intelligence was not lifeless. I will not quote passages here to

28

show that Scott had the power to think deeply about such questions as the relation between society and the individual, or historical causation, or the conflict of cultures. For the chapters that follow are dedicated to demonstrating just that. I shall rather ask the reader to take it for a moment on trust. If this is accepted, then it will surely be clear that neither the English nor the Scots could be spared. For him the analytical English paragraphs were the way of coming to understand, assimilate and judge the strong, and sometimes wild emotions expressed by his characters in the vernacular. Unless a novel makes a pattern, it is no more than a set of anecdotes. Meg Merrilies, Baron Bradwardine and the rest, need not only to be felt but to be understood. Scott's dual method ensures that they are.

2 *The Two Voices*

Scott stands apart from his great contemporaries by being so much more like a man of the ordinary world. He showed none of Wordsworth's passionate belief in the spiritual grandeur of art, none of the strange quality of the sage that impressed those who met Coleridge,[1] none of Keats' curiosity about the character of the aesthetic experience. His attitude to his art hovered between the engaging modesty of the successful author who 'really does not know what all the fuss is about' and honest philistine joy in a notable professional success. The first impulse is well seen in his daughter's famous reply that she hadn't read *The Lady of the Lake* because 'Papa says there's nothing so bad for young people as reading bad poetry.'[2] The second is responsible for his rapidity and carelessness.

If, as this book assumes, Scott was also a great writer, it is obvious that the incurious, 'plain man' approach could have odd results. For he wrote in a time when it was no longer possible to accept one's own place in the literary tradition without reflection as one accepts the agreed customs of society. In a literary scene which contains Wordsworth, Coleridge, Crabbe, Keats, Byron, Peacock and Jane Austen there can be no agreed customs. Being himself a very complex man, not being an introspective man, he was bound to

[1] See, for instance, Carlyle's *Life of Sterling* chap VIII.
[2] *Lockhart* III 267.

oscillate strangely. It is an odd thought that for the Victorians his reputation rested largely on works that seem today quite secondary—works like *Marmion* and *Ivanhoe*.

If we want an example of this oscillation at its most violent we may turn to the end of *Guy Mannering*, and to the extraordinary change that comes over the story between chapter 49 and chapter 50. The central idea, of a young man returning to the home of his ancestors, knowing nothing of his own connection with it, could be treated in many ways. Scott is shyly aware of mythical and metaphysical possibilities, when he writes, at the end of chapter 40, "Thus, unconscious as the most absolute stranger . . . without the countenance of a friend within the circle of several hundred miles; accused of a heavy crime, and what was as bad as all the rest, being nearly penniless, did the harassed wanderer for the first time, after the interval of so many years, approach the remains of the castle where his ancestors had exercised all but regal dominion." I say shyly because prosaic words like 'penniless' seem at the same time to insist on a thoroughly worldly, common-sense interpretation. And the passage omitted above is even more prosaic: it runs: "in circumstances, which, if not destitute, were for the present highly embarrassing." We seem to be half in the world of factual narrative, and half in the world of Wordsworth's Immortality ode, and 'that imperial palace whence he came'.

But, of course, there is another possible way of treating the story, far from either of these. There is also the makings of a good old eighteenth century melodrama, with wills, long-lost heirs and startling coincidences. This is the big bow-wow strain, which as Scott pleasantly remarked on another occasion he could do as well as anybody. How to reconcile all three, psychological myth, logical narrative, melodramatic thrill?

The answer is that it can't be done, and Scott knew it. So, by the quotation he placed at the head of chapter 50, he threw up the sponge. It comes from Sheridan's *The Critic*, and it runs:

> *Justice.* This does indeed confirm each circumstance
> The gipsy told!
> No orphan, nor without a friend art thou:
> *I* am thy father, *here's* thy mother, *there*
> Thy uncle, *this* thy first cousin, and *these*
> Are all thy near relations!

If we have responded to the potential grandeur of the theme, this comes as a betrayal. Worse, Meg Merrilies has been transformed into this absurd gipsy. Here, it is not only we who are betrayed, it is Scott too. For we know from the passage of self-criticism, quoted above,[1] that Scott saw in Meg Merrilies one of his finest achievements. We ask, how could he guy his own best work at the very time of writing?

We know that *Guy Mannering*, his second novel, was much less carefully considered than his first. Its connection with its ostensible source, the verse story of the astrologer,[2] is perfunctory. No doubt Scott, conscious of being at the height of his powers, conscious of untapped intellectual energies stored up in the years before his major works began, imagined when he began that all difficulties would dissolve in the process of composition as they had in *Waverley*.

We have seen how, even when expressing the highest enthusiasm for his own portrayal of Meg Merrilies,[1] he spoke in the old-fashioned sensible terms. We are here at the heart of the problem raised by all feelings and all literary effects of exceptional intensity. As T. S. Eliot said, commenting on Arnold's 'Poetry is at bottom a criticism of life': "At the bottom of the abyss is what few ever see and what those cannot bear to look at for long; and it is not a 'criticism of

---

[1] Chap 1.   [2] See *Lockhart* V, 5.

life'."[1] Whether poetry is at bottom a criticism of life I do not know. But the phrase seems to be a very fair summary of what is achieved by our great novelists. How is the glimpse of 'the abyss' to be incorporated in the critical structure?

For Scott this was much more than a problem of literary technique. It involved a whole problem of living. He had the sorrowful opportunity in watching his friend Byron to study the nemesis of the search for perpetual intensity. The easy, middling, humdrum things that Byron despised he did not despise. In the ordinary concerns of life, in society, in politics, even to some extent in reading, he gloried in being a conventional man.

It is startling to compare his intensely sympathetic treatment of the gipsies evicted by Godfrey Bertram with the usual tone of his correspondence on the subject of riots, civil disorders, and disreputable unemployed persons. Scott was sometimes reckless and slapdash; he was never, I believe, insincere. There is no need to suspect, in his case, what might seem plausible enough in another, that he kept his anarchic sentiments strictly for fiction where they could do no harm, but in life always spoke as a man with a stake in the country. Each impulse was a genuine part of his nature, and both are to be found in his imaginative and in his practical life. The contrast comes because they are mixed in different proportions; and, in *Guy Mannering* at least, the anarchic and romantic strain is easily dominant. But not as completely dominant as one is apt to think if one is relying on memory; for Meg Merrilies and Harry Bertram's homecoming are unforgettable. It is easier to underrate the importance of chapters 42-3, with its very Augustan satire on the way Justices of the Peace administer the law. ('Sir Robert, who would almost have died of shame at committing such a

[1] T. S. Eliot: *The Use of Poetry and the Use of Criticism*, 1933 p111.

solecism as sending a captain of horse to jail . . .') We are apt to forget too that when Dominie Sampson calls Meg Merrilies 'harlot, thief, witch and gipsy', he is not necessarily a narrow-minded bigot, but is giving a true though incomplete statement of the case.

In one celebrated scene, more clearly perhaps than anywhere else in his works, the two Scotts confront each other. This is part of the reason for its obscure depth of emotional appeal. The justly famous speech beginning 'Ride your ways, Laird of Ellangowan'[1] has been quoted and analysed sufficiently, and on this point I have nothing to add. But it has not generally been noticed that this speech is only the climax of a subtle and carefully-modulated chapter. In preceding chapters we have seen enough of Bertram to understand both his character and circumstances, and I must emphasize, of course, that the likeness I see to one aspect of Scott's mind is specialized and not general. Bertram is as unlike Scott as possible in being dull, lazy and fond of grievances. His conduct towards the gipsies has been prepared for in an earlier chapter where he expresses his resentment at not being a Justice of the Peace, an appointment which he considers the traditional due of the laird. When at last he receives the appointment, he does what all stupid, indolent men do on obtaining a coveted appointment—he sets up as a new broom, and clears off the gipsies. It is important here, I think, to try to capture for a moment that everyday practical mentality by which we live most of our lives, but which most of us leave behind while reading imaginative literature. The gipsies are a threat to discipline, tidiness and good order. Bertram has the law on his side. He is not a cruel man; merely like many people in authority, fussy, opinionated and self-important.

In his description of Meg Merrilies poised to deliver her

[1] *Guy Mannering* chap 8.

magnificent tirade, the shrewd, sceptical side of Scott's complex character is in the ascendant:

'She was standing upon one of those high precipitous banks, which, as we have before noticed, overhung the road; so that she was placed considerably higher than Ellangowan, even though he was on horseback; and her tall figure, relieved against the clear blue sky, seemed almost of supernatural stature. We have noticed that there was in her general attire, or rather in her mode of adjusting it, somewhat of a foreign costume, artfully adopted perhaps for the purpose of adding to the effect of her spells and predictions, or perhaps from some traditional notions respecting the dress of her ancestors. On this occasion, she had a large piece of red cotton cloth rolled about her head in the form of a turban, from beneath which her dark eyes flashed with uncommon lustre. Her long and tangled hair fell in elf-locks from the folds of this singular headgear. Her attitude was that of a sibyl in frenzy, and she stretched out, in her right hand, a sapling bough which seemed just pulled."

The approach here is external and analytical. He does not tell us what she was thinking; he deduces as much as he can about her motives from her appearance and conduct and from known traditions. He writes, in fact, very much like what he was, a lawyer. Even the phrases which do not at first seem to fit this role, like 'supernatural stature,' and 'sibyl in frenzy' are not altogether exceptions. For they are distanced. The tone is, 'Gentlemen of the jury, you may have seen in the City Art Gallery compositions of a classical and antique character. Well, these will give you a good idea . . .'

But the really surprising thing about the passage, and one easily forgotten in the excitement of the great speech that immediately follows, is the degree of deliberate artifice it ascribes to Meg Merrilies. The prudent lawyer is warning us against the witness. Then the witness speaks, and we promptly forget the warning. For she speaks with a heart-breaking

35

eloquence and truth. The Edinburgh lawyer in Scott, the plain everyday self in the reader is routed as easily as Meg Merrilies in her moment of disgrace annihilates Bertram.

Now, for a time, in what follows Scott deals very ably with the problem of incorporating the glimpse of the abyss into the criticism of life. Meg's connection with the Bertram family goes much deeper than her simple function as the protector of the young hero when his identity is unknown to himself and his family. She aspires to be the guardian of the whole family tradition; she does not resent Bertram's authority as the laird. On the contrary, she despises him as a weak and forgetful steward. He is not traditional, not feudal enough. It is Meg, not Bertram who cries, 'Wha durst buy Ellangowan that was not of Bertram's blude?'[1] It is very characteristic of Scott to give his strange prophetic rebel against authority a conservative tinge.

When Meg speaks, Scott cannot help being on her side, any more than we can. Yet Bertram comes very near to important aspects of the author's ordinary self, when, nonplussed by her energy and indignation, feebly stirred to ineffective regrets, he "was clearing his voice to speak, and thrusting his hand in his pocket to find a half-crown; the gipsy waited neither for his reply nor his donation." This is a moment of profound significance; and it is notable that for all his celebrated prolixity as a describer of detail, Scott's deepest insights are breathtaking in their brevity and their dramatic force. For here we have an image of a strong current in eighteenth century thought; here is necessary social change (enclosures, say, or Highland clearances) tempered by a manly benevolence. Half a crown would have been no contemptible sum to the gipsies. In the person of Bertram, all those progressive-conservative, kindly, class-conscious men, of whom Sir Walter Scott was so notable a

[1] Chap 22.

representative, are contemptuously brushed aside without a word.

He does not leave the stark opposition altogether without judicial comment. But in order to avoid anti-climax, he gives it beforehand: "The race, it is true, which he had thus summarily dismissed from their ancient place of refuge, was idle and vicious; but had he endeavoured to render them otherwise? They were not more irregular characters now, than they had been while they were admitted to consider themselves as a sort of subordinate dependents of his family; and ought the mere circumstance of his becoming a magistrate to have made at once such a change in his conduct towards them? Some means of reformation ought at least to have been tried, before sending seven families at once upon the wide world, and depriving them of a degree of countenance, which withheld them at least from atrocious guilt."

This passage is not a highly distinguished one; but it is enough to prevent for the time a total opposition between the prophetic and the workaday world.

Yes, it is a sensible and humane comment, yet it does not altogether satisfy us. For we may think, how can he *dare* to speak to Meg Merrilies like that? She has raised herself far beyond the range of his pity or ours.

Yet Meg Merrilies' prophetic voice presents a less serious threat to the novel's coherence than Harry Bertram's homecoming. For in describing the latter, what is needed is not eloquent speech in a moment of crisis, but a deep psychological analysis, and perhaps a symbolic interpretation. There was a personal shyness about Scott, a natural reluctance to be introspective, a distrust of philosophic profundity; he found himself unwilling to probe too deeply into the inner meaning of his own story when, as here, it had strong mythical possibilities. So, while the prophetic voice of Meg Merrilies only makes the foundations creak, Harry Bertram's return brings the structure tumbling down; and the collapse is signalized by the quotation from Sheridan already given, followed by a hasty, shamefaced, touchingly absurd conclusion.

II

The end of *Guy Mannering* is, of course, a failure. But it is an instructive failure, and one that gives promise of high success on other occasions. It is the failure of a *multiple* man, a man with several contrary strains in his artistic personality. The second half of this book will discuss the masterpieces in which the harmony is achieved, and all the conflicting strains reconciled. Here I want to deal with a narrower question, the implications of class-conflict in Scott's two voices. If we take Scott's life and writings as a whole, there is an obvious paradox in his class attitudes. Really by nature and by training a professional man, he ruined himself in the insatiable thirst for a castle, broad acres and aristocratic status. No one responded more strongly than he to the grandeur of a famous family name, the romance of royalty, the pride of blood and heraldry. Yet no novelist before him, and very few since, have conveyed with such feeling the dignity of the poor, the disreputable, the mad and the outcast. When these two strong impulses clash, it is nearly always the second that conquers, just as Meg Merrilies conquered the laird.

But it is not always, as it is there, an open conflict, and a decisive victory. There are times when a delicate humour takes the place of these. A scene in *Old Mortality* provides a significant example. Lady Margaret Bellenden enacts repetitively and a little woodenly the role of the worshipper of royalty. Charles II once visited her house, and she will keep on telling of 'His Sacred Majesty's disjune' and the glorious cushion on which the King sat. Then, in chapter 28, the servant Jenny tells Morton: "A'body says thay you and

38

the whigs hae made a vow to ding King Charles aff the throne, and that neither he, nor his posteriors from generation to generation, shall sit upon it ony mair . . ."

At first sight we may think we have here one of those uneducated errors in language which have made good fun from the mechanicals in *A Midsummer Night's Dream* to Fielding's Partridge and beyond. But this is not so, for Jenny means, of course, descendants when she says 'posteriors'; and the use of the word in this sense is perfectly correct.[1] But at the same time, she is unconsciously parodying her mistress's obsessive concern for trivial physical details in her worship of royalty. Jenny says by mistake what Lady Margaret means but is too well-bred to say, that the great thing is to have the King's buttocks on your cushion. When we understand this we see that Scott is really giving us a most significant reversal of the tradition of the comic servant. It is the aristocratic lady who has the low, physical conception. It is the uneducated servant who has the more elevated political idea. Lady Margaret, not Jenny, is made to look ridiculous by Jenny's accidental pun.

Class feeling is a subject that lends itself easily to humbug. Nothing is more certain than that kind hearts are more than coronets, yet we always feel uneasy when we hear someone solemnly pronouncing the fact. Very often the self-deception is entirely honest and unconscious. The wealthy advocates of comprehensive schools always have a particularly good and convincing reason for putting the boy down for Eton. Almost everyone, in theory, is on the side of the poor against the rich. Now the curious thing about Scott is that with him the self-deception works just the other way. As a man of the world of conservative views, fearful of the mob, and in his last year or two dreading the passage of the Reform Bill,

[1] The OED dates the meaning *descendants* from 1534, and the meaning *buttocks* from 1605.

Scott identified himself with the interests of the ruling class. But when he forgets his public personality, it is different. In his jokes a man is most himself. Jenny's triumph over Lady Margaret is from this point of view perhaps even more significant than the triumph of Meg Merrilies. It is so natural, so uncontrived. It comes from one of the author's primary impulses, anterior to consciously-held opinion.

If the two voices contribute to the richness and fascination of Scott's work at its best, there are times when they only increase its confusion. Sometimes he just presents us with two opposite opinions, one expressed dramatically, the other by author's comment. Take for instance this passage where a rustic is speaking of the disreputable George Staunton:

" 'And yet 'tis pity on Master George, too,' " continued the honest boor, 'for he has an open hand, and winna let a poor body want an he has it'.

The virtue of profuse generosity, by which, indeed, they themselves are most directly advantaged, is readily admitted by the vulgar as a cloak for many sins"[1]

'Only by the vulgar?' one is tempted to ask. Was St. Peter's epistle written by one of the 'vulgar'? Scott is not really thinking here. The two parts of his mind are each giving an automatic response; there is no interaction, and so no development and no real interest for the reader. At moments like this, the most warm-hearted of men can sound cold. But there are other passages, much more significant for us, when there is a satisfying synthesis. One of these is the burial of Steenie Mucklebackit in chapter 31 of *The Antiquary*. We see at one and the same time that the reckless expenditure of the poor on funerals is illogical and vain, and that is is salutary and deeply comforting. Few things are so difficult to describe and judge as the irrational traditions of a class or culture different from one's own. It is so easy and so

[1] *The Heart of Midlothian* chap 34.

inadequate to be narrowly utilitarian, or coolly scientific, or sentimentally antiquarian. Scott here avoids all these pitfalls partly because he is strongly moved by all three impulses. But he has a simpler primary impulse too, to mourn with those that mourn. And this is anterior to all sociological enquiries, and all economic judgments. Here the simplicity of one of the most intellectually complex of men fuses together all the contrary types of judgment he can make. We are able to see the living force of custom, its power to support the mind in unbearable moments. In passages like this there is a perfect reconciliation of the very conflicting impulses and standards which caused the collapse at the end of *Guy Mannering*. When we read them we would not have Scott a more single-minded man, a 'purer' artist, than he was. The contradictions in his personality and often in his literary aims were necessary for these rich achievements.

Here, once again, all the artistic intensity is given to the poor. In this chapter, the antiquary, very near in some ways to Scott himself, feels all the sensible kindly objections to unnecessary expenditure that the Laird of Abbotsford would no doubt have felt in the case of a poor tenant. He is right, in a way, but the needy slaves of custom and pride are seen to be much more deeply right. Once again as in the case of Jenny and Lady Margaret Bellenden, we feel that an irresistible force of artistic sincerity has given a verdict, which the decent, conventional man of the world could not have given.

3 *The Prophetic and the Social*

So far we have been considering less the novels themselves than the impulses behind them. It is now time to examine the artistic consequences of Scott's double vision. Meg Merrilies is not alone in possessing the prophetic fire. Edie Ochiltree,[1] Madge Wildfire,[2] the aged Alice[3] and Norna[4] are strongly endued, while others like Magdalen Graeme[5] and Lord Glenallan[6] have occasional or momentary visitations.

All these, either habitually or temporarily, speak as if they had put the ordinary common sense of the world away from them. The reasons for this vary, and there is little similarity of content in what they say. But the point that links them once and for all in our minds is this. What they say is unanswerable, self-justifying. They seem to have a footing outside time, an authority that society can neither give nor take away.

Moreover, this authority is impersonal. It does not derive from saintliness, from grandeur of mind or power of will. It is consistent with craziness, with roguery, and even, in Glenallan's case with weak timidity. But though the authority is impersonal, the idiom is intensely personal. It would be impossible to interchange the speeches between one possessor of the prophetic voice and another. The prophetic voice

[1] *The Antiquary.*   [2] *The Heart of Midlothian.*
[3] *The Bride of Lammermoor.*   [4] *The Pirate.*   [5] *The Abbot.*
[6] *The Antiquary.*

mingles with the actual language, motives and circumstances of the speaker. The practical effect of what is said depends on the whole logic of the story. Even in this strange territory, Scott walks as a novelist above all. Though each is capable, at times, of criticizing the agreed conventions of society, none of them ever gives the impression of speaking the author's own view from a point outside the action. The prophetic voice is far from that easy determination to set the world to rights, an author's lecture transmitted through a character that we find, for instance, in the plays of Bernard Shaw. Thus Madge Wildfire speaks as she does because she has been driven to distraction by society's rejection of the 'fallen woman'. Alice can predict the fate of the Ravenswoods partly because she remembers so much of their forgotten history, in which the causes of future events were prepared. Edie Ochiltree can see the absurdity of duelling because it has never been a vice of his own class. Lord Glenallan's timidity and seclusion give him time for the solitary brooding in which he perceives the wickedness of war. Norna is a professional fortune-teller whose trade encourages petty dishonesties and Delphic evasions, and in her the genuine prophetic voice is heard intermittently, while the false professional knowingness is never at a loss.

I take Edie Ochiltree first. We see him first in a scene which emphasizes his broad, humorous earthiness, a quality in which the others are more or less lacking. Oldbuck, the antiquary, is explaining to Lovel about the fascinating local remains, when a voice from behind interrupts: "Praetorian here, Praetorian there, I mind the bigging o' it." Then we are given a balanced account of the class to which Edie belongs, the 'Blue-gown' or professional beggar.[1] Of course, Edie is right, and the Roman remains are nonsense.

Edie's next scene comes when Sir Arthur Wardour and

---

[1] *The Antiquary* chap 4.

his daughter Isabella are threatened with destruction by the abnormal tide as they walk on the sands below the great cliffs. Sir Arthur, a magistrate and important local land-owner, has just directed the constables 'to take up that scoundrelly old beggar Edie Ochiltree, for spreading dis-affection against church and state'. Now he and his daughter are met by Edie striding across the sands and warning them that they will be drowned if they continue on the way they have chosen, and the danger is nearly as great if they turn back.

" 'Good man' said Sir Arthur, 'can you think of nothing? —of no help?—I'll make you rich—I'll give you a farm— I'll——' 'Our riches will be soon equal', said the beggar, looking out upon the strife of the waters—'they are sae already; for I hae nae land, and you would give your fair bounds and barony for a square yard of rock that would be dry for twal hours.' " And a little later, when a possible way of escape up the cliff-face has been found, and Sir Arthur commands Isabella to stay with him, Edie says: " 'Lordsake, Sir Arthur, haud your tongue, and be thankful to God that there's wiser folk than you to manage this job.' "

When the rescue is completed, and Oldbuck comes to greet the Wardours and reward Edie, he replies: " 'Na, Na! I never tak gowd—besides, Monkbarns,[1] ye wad maybe be rueing it the morn.' Then turning to the group of fishermen and peasants, 'Now, sirs, wha will gie me a supper and some clean pease-strae?' "[2]

Edie's precise relation to a settled class-system is here very easy to misunderstand. Scott lived in a time of revolution, and the year 1789 found him at the impressionable age of eighteen. As a citizen and public man he fully concurred in the severity of the aristocratic reaction against revolutionary

[1] Monkbarns is a territorial title of Jonathan Oldbuck.
[2] *The Antiquary* chaps 7 and 8.

tendencies which dominated the English political scene for most of his adult life. It is tempting perhaps to see Edie as a licensed rebel against the class system, one who gives the psychological release provided in earlier times by fools and jesters. But in some ways, Edie is as staunch a conservative as Sir Arthur Wardour himself. He accepts the class-system, and he by no means conceives himself as an outcast from society. He speaks plainly and at times rudely to his betters because that is his nature, because plain-speaking is an accepted feature of Scots tradition, and also because moments of crisis make everyday distinctions irrelevant.

Moreover, he has a clear idea of his own social function. A little later, when Isabella offers to pension him off and give him a regular lodging, which he has never had, he speaks of his traditional duty of carrying news, and passing on lore about the treatment of cattle in illness, and says: " 'I canna lay down my vocation; it would be a public loss.' "[1] In the passage quoted just now, when he refuses gold, the motive is not really proud plebeian independence, nor resentment at being paid for an act of humanity, nor self-denial. He is acting on system; he feels that it will be to his own loss in the long run if his privileged status as a beggar, who never accepts more than will suffice for the day, is eroded by the acceptance of larger gifts. In his own eyes he is a working member of society whose remuneration is willingly and justly provided, as we are told, mostly by people very little richer than himself. Yet in Wardour's eyes he is an offensive vagabond, who should be punished by law, just as Meg Merrilies was to Bertram.

If we read on to discover which view of Edie, his own or Wardour's, is correct, we are likely to be puzzled. His moment of authority comes when a duel is fought: 'What are ye come here for, young men? are ye come amongst the most

[1] Chap 12.

lovely works of God to break His laws? Have ye left the works of man, the houses and cities that are but clay and dust, like those that built them; and are ye come here among the peaceful hills, and by the quiet waters, that will last whiles aught earthly shall endure, to destroy each other's lives, that will have but an unco short time, by the course of nature, to make up a lang account at the close o't? O Sirs! hae ye brothers, sisters, fathers, that hae tended ye, and mothers that hae travailed for ye, friends that hae ca'd ye like a piece o' their ain heart? And is this the way ye tak to make them childless and brotherless and friendless? Ohon! it's an ill feight whar he that wins has the warst o't."[1]

We can have no doubt about the authority conveyed by this powerful amalgam of moral truth, biblical eloquence and peasant shrewdness, which is set against the petty reply of one of the principals, who complains that if they listen to this advice, they "would rise the next morning with reputations as ragged as our friend here, who has obliged us with a rather unnecessary display of his oratory." Yet we may wonder whether Scott's sense of fitness has deserted him when we find Edie's exhortation immediately preceded by an undignified begging scene; and a little later he speaks of the way he has practised on Oldbuck's credulity in the past, and of his need to keep a secret hiding-place, because although he trusts 'in the power o' grace that I'll ne'er do ony thing to need ane again, yet naebody kens what temptation ane may be gien ower to'. What are we to make of a man who speaks one moment like a humorous old rogue, and the next like a prophet, who has an eye for profit and advantage yet refuses gold, a beggar who at one moment takes an offer of money as an insult, a vagabond who has a strong sense of the dignity of his social position?

To answer this we need to consider all the circumstances

[1] Chap 20.

of Edie's great moment of authority in the speech quoted above. The practice of duelling is as full of paradox as Edie's own position. How can a custom be at the same time a requirement of honour, a privilege of gentlemen and a moral outrage, a clear denial of the unquestioned religious bases of society? The paradoxes balance, though one is so familiar as to have lost its edge for Scott's characters, and perhaps for his readers, until Edie recalls it.

Scott was in every possible sense of the word a social man. No one less than he could have gone into the desert to fast and pray. No one was more aware that irrational custom has practical value. No one had more respect for the traditional ordering of society. There can be no question of Edie exposing society as a sham, no question even of Lovel, the hero, suffering seriously in the author's eyes or in ours for fighting a duel. Yet something deep in Scott felt that all traditional customs and distinctions were from a certain point of view nugatory. It was a point of view that he seldom, if ever, cared to adopt in his daily life. One can read through his volumes of correspondence and find scarcely a hint of it. But the impulse to adopt this point of view, though deeply veiled, was strong. No one can doubt that these prophetic passages are written with the full force of artistic sincerity. Through Edie Ochiltree, he could do what in everyday, common-sense terms was, perhaps, impossible. He could reconcile the two sides of his nature. Edie is both strongly-rooted in society, like the everyday Scott, and possessed of the prophetic voice. And typically, this prophetic voice is also traditional; it returns both to the religious sources of our culture, and to the unanswerable voice of reason in human affairs. Duels are, more obviously than any other practice, an uncivilized inclusion embedded in the customs of civilized life. Edie, the outsider is also the insider; just as much as Wordsworth's Old Cumberland Beggar he is a member of the living body of society, with a function, and a re-

47

ward which is meagre, but can be accepted with dignity.

Here the prophetic and the everyday are reconciled in one character possessed of the reconciling power of a great poetic image. But it is not always so. Norna in *The Pirate* is a less carefully finished portrait than Edie, for *The Pirate* comes in a period of Scott's life when he had begun to write hurriedly, and when careless melodramatic elements are sometimes found entwined round the story that matters to the author and to us. Nevertheless, the partial likeness to Edie, and the partial contrast possess a great interest.

It is important to notice, first, that *The Pirate* has a geographical setting with which Scott was only slightly acquainted. Drawn outside his normal range by the northerness of the Orkneys and Shetlands, and by the hints of a Nordic culture alien to the Scotland he knew, Scott wrote sketchily about matters which he usually grasped very firmly: society, tradition, economics. Inevitably, then, Norna as a weird prophetess is less exactly placed than Edie. It is not always clear how far she is a strange exception in the eyes of the surrounding people, and how far she is a typical product of an exotic society. But what is quite certain is that Scott is in a much more critical, rationalistic mood as he writes of her. We may be uneasy when we read: " 'I say to you beware; while Norna looks forth at the measureless waters from the crest of Fitful Head, something is yet left that resembles power of defence. If the men of Thule have ceased to be champions, and to spread the banquet for the raven, the women have not forgotten the arts that lifted them of yore into queens and prophetesses.' "[1] For this is surely a bit 'literary', as if, which was indeed probably the case, Scott had not fully assimilated and had time to reflect upon new Nordic studies. And to those who have really experienced the strange and satisfying originality of Edie Ochiltree, it

[1] *The Pirate* chap 5.

would be painful to have the model vulgarized. But then Scott embarks on a most intelligent analysis of the change in public attitudes to people supposed to possess preternatural powers, as society develops, and adds: "In our days, it would have been questioned whether she was an impostor, or whether her imagination was so deeply impressed with the mysteries of her supposed art that she might be in some degree a believer in her own pretensions to supernatural knowledge." This is almost the voice of Hume.

But Scott could never play Hume for long, for in his depths he responded to the power of the irrational which his Scottish predecessors of the eighteenth century found it so easy to dismiss. In the very next chapter she speaks without Nordic paraphernalia, without praeternatural claims, with an authority akin to Edie Ochiltree's. Having eaten a meal grudgingly given by cheeseparing hosts she says: " 'I give you no thanks . . . I pay you with what you will value more than the gratitude of the whole inhabitants of Hialtland. Say not that Norna of Fitful Head hath eaten of your bread and drunk of your cup, and left you sorrowing for the charge to which she hath put your house.' So saying, she laid on the table a small piece of antique gold coin, bearing the rude and half-defaced effigies of some ancient Northern king." Here we have, as with Edie, the proud claim of the outcast and beggar to subsistence as his due; and the claim is implicitly admitted by society, for her hosts, mean-spirited and churlish though they are, speak of the payment as an 'everlasting shame to us.'

In chapter 7 we find her doing just what Edie did, intervening with unanswerable authority to prevent a quarrel that might have been fatal. But the difference in the result is significant. Edie, speaking with a prophetic voice inspired only by truth and reason, found his words unheeded; Norna's darker authority, with its suspicion of witchcraft, at least for the time prevails. Like Edie denouncing the duel,

Norna is here rebuking a usage sanctioned by popular consent and tradition, but inherently barbarous. For the
islanders believe that it is unlucky to help the victims of
shipwreck; and so we have the paradox that the threatening
authority of the dark powers supposed to be embodied in
Norna is needed to enforce a precept of ordinary humanity.
There could not be a neater way of showing that the irrational has depths undreamed of by the Edinburgh Augustans, and that it is altogether closer than they thought to the
moral centre of our being.

We have seen that Norna, unlike all her peers in prophecy,
is a professional prophet. Just as the crazy Madge Wildfire
or the feeble Alice can be unconsciously inspired, so the professional prophet must live in the workaday world, suffer
all its blows, and be infected by its errors and deceits. Her
power to use the authority of the irrational for high ends of
charity does not prevent her from practising deception, or
from being weighed down with the burden of sin. At one
moment she denies with horror the charge of having sold her
soul to the devil; at others she is not averse from deriving
profit from this awful reputation.

Her conception of guilt is fragmentary and inconsistent
like all her thinking. In chapter 8 she speaks with obvious
sincerity of sin, redemption and retribution in Christian
terms. But she is also influenced by pagan images of guilt as a
stain inflicted by destiny without any conscious act. Thus she
refers to herself as a parricide because a chance action, entirely innocent of intent, appears to have contributed to her
father's death.

How far Scott was giving a fair account of conditions in
the Orkney and Shetland islands about 1700 may be doubtful. But in general terms Norna embodies a most interesting
idea, which adds richness to Scott's whole treatment of the
prophetic voice. He is showing us here that if the prophetic
voice could react on society, it was equally inevitable that

the assumptions of society should affect the functioning of the prophetic voice. The northern islands are pictured in *The Pirate* as lacking consistency about fundamentals. The population cannot distinguish the sources of their various beliefs. They are sincerely Christian and sincerely pagan. They believe in Norna as a purveyor of dark magical powers, but they are also able to be profoundly impressed when she speaks with a genuine, 'non-professional' prophetic voice. They do not consciously distinguish between the two, any more than they distinguish what belongs to faith and what to local superstitions in their religious customs. Just as Browning's Mr. Sludge was a cheat, and yet a genuine believer in the psychic phenomena which were his stock-in-trade, so Norna's prophetic voice is partly corrupted but not stifled by her position as magician to the neighbourhood.

So Norna stands for an important general truth about the relation between prophecy and society. Society is based on an unanalysable amalgam of principles, interests and customs. Moral criticism or extramoral prophetic criticism can justly attack its assumptions. But the voice of authority can only speak with the words and ideas that society gives. The islanders, perhaps, are incapable of hearing the prophetic voice unless the speaker is encumbered by the authority of a traditional superstition. For Scott, those who defend customs simply because they are venerable and stabilizing forces in society, and those who attack them only because they are not reasonable are both wide of the mark. The most social of men and of novelists, he was aware of strange hidden links between unlike things.

But if Norna's prophetic voice can be (partly) corrupted, Edie Ochiltree's can be surprisingly superseded. The prophetic power passes for a moment from him to Lord Glenallan.

" 'What was your trade in your youth?' continued the Earl.

'A soldier, my lord; and mony a sair day's kemping I've seen. I was to have been made a sergeant, but——'

'A soldier! then you have slain and burnt, and sacked and spoiled?'

'I winna say,' replied Edie, 'that I have been better than my neighbours—it's a rough trade—war's sweet to them that never tried it.'

'And you are now old and miserable, asking from precarious charity the food which in your youth you tore from the hands of the poor peasant?'

'I am a beggar, it is true, my lord; but I am nae just sae miserable neither. For my sins, I hae grace to repent of them, if I might say sae, and to lay them where they may be better borne than by me; and for my food, naebody grudges an auld man a bit and a drink. Sae I live as I can, and am contented to die when I am ca'd upon.'

'And thus, then, with little to look back upon that is pleasant or praiseworthy in your past life, with less to look forward to on this side of eternity, you are contented to drag out the rest of your existence—Go, begone; and in your age and poverty and weariness never envy the lord of such a mansion as this, either in his sleeping or his waking moments—Here is something for thee.' "[1]

Edie is so startled at the voice of authority being used against him that though he refused Oldbuck's money, he now accepts the extraordinary gift of five or six guineas.

We know Edie well enough by now to know that he is not overawed by rank. Lord Glenallan speaks here not with the authority of rank but with the authority of great suffering. The strange family secrets that are supposed to account for the suffering may be melodramatic and unconvincing. But that does not matter here. For here is the authentic note of

[1] *The Antiquary* chap 28.

a man driven by suffering and solitary brooding to question the general assumptions of society.

Edie Ochiltree remains in the book as a whole a far more convincing and memorable figure than Glenallan. But the effect of this one short passage on our whole idea of Edie is considerable. Edie is in some ways a conventional man. He is honest enough not to pretend that war is enjoyable, but he has failed, just as society in general has failed, to perceive the wickedness of the trade of soldier of fortune, because war is a traditional pursuit of all classes, while duelling is not. Lord Glenallan sees something about war that Edie does not, but is quite unaware of the incongruity of deriving five hundred a year from a place he has never heard of.

So Scott's prophetic voice is never irrevocably incarnated in a single person. It is as if no one could detach himself completely enough from the clogging but life-giving earthiness of society to be wholly prophetic or wholly rational or wholly Christian. 'Give me a place to stand and I will move the earth.' Scott and all his characters know that they cannot in the end move the earth because they must stand on it, and no writer's earth is more earthy than Scott's. But it is possible for some of his characters, intermittently, to stand as it were on a high mountain and see the pattern of society from a distance. Seen thus it looks strange, and some markings are visible which cannot be discerned by those who walk across them in the fields below. The rare moments when this happens affect the whole impression made by Scott's work and our view of the man. For the most social of novelists society is always necessary, but never an absolute. Both Edie and Glenallan are part of the society they criticize. They are not prophets by nature, but they have moments of insight when they can speak with the prophetic voice.

Society is not an absolute, because it is always changing. The assumptions of one age are the laughing-stock of another. Scott is at his best when he can show two different societies in conflict, as in *The Highland Widow* and *The Two Drovers*. These two stories come late in Scott's career, in *The Chronicles of the Canongate* (1827), and may be regarded as his last works of distinction. The series in which they were included was also the first volume of prose fiction published without any pretence of anonymity, and was written in the immediate aftermath of the great crash of 1825. In the mass of inferior work, which haste, fatigue and insolvency fostered in his late years they have a peculiar interest.

The Highland Widow is set a few years after the Jacobite rising of 1745, and is thus almost contemporary in its historical setting with *Redgauntlet*. In outline it is a simple story of a young Highlander who finds that only one way of advancement is open to him, when the traditional society in which his father lived is shattered by the consequences of the defeat of the '45. He must join the British army, but his widowed mother is convinced that this would be a betrayal of his ancestors. He comes home to her remote cottage on his last leave, explaining to her that if he does not arrive at the depot at Dumbarton at the appointed time he will be treated as a deserter. She asks scornfully what is the punishment of a deserter.

" 'Mother,' said Hamish, 'it signifies little to what a criminal may be exposed, if a man is determined not to be such. Our Highland chiefs used also to punish their vassals, and, as I have heard, severely.—Was it not Lachlan MacIan, whom we remember of old, whose head was struck off by order of his chieftain for shooting at the stag before him?'

'Ay,' said Elspat, 'and right he had to lose it, since he dishonoured the father of the people even in the face of the assembled clan. But the chiefs were noble in their ire— they punished with the sharp blade and not with the baton. Their punishments drew blood, but they did not infer dishonour. Canst thou say the same for the laws under whose yoke thou hast placed thy freeborn neck?'

'I cannot—mother—I cannot', said Hamish, mournfully. 'I saw them punish a Sassenach for deserting, as they called it, his banner. He was scourged—I own it—scourged like a hound who has offended an imperious master. I was sick at the sight—I confess it. But the punishment of dogs is only for those worse than dogs, who know not how to keep their faith.' "[1]

Perhaps in his prime Scott would have found more telling words in a few of these sentences; for instance 'infer' seems rather a bookish word for the widow to use. Nevertheless, the essential situation is sharp and clear, and it would be quite wrong to be misled by the apparent triviality of the distinction between one physical instrument of punishment and another. The real distinction which both feel but which the widow cannot explain, because she is unused to abstract distinctions, is between legal punishment and arbitrary power. Thus the comparative leniency of a flogging as against a beheading is part of the ground of offence. The savage punishment of beheading is acceptable because it is performed in anger. Being the product of strong feeling it does not break the bonds of clan loyalty. The only thing that would break them would be the spirit of calculation, and of this a set of written rules and codified punishments for stated offences are in the eyes of these two an ominous example.

That the widow's actual account of these feelings is so inadequate, and yet that the young man should feel an echo of her inner thought in his own mind—this is exactly right. It shows Hamish for what he is, not a traitor to the family tradition, not the first of the generation of new men who are assimilated into an alien society without difficulty, but an-

[1] *The Highland Widow* chap 4.

other version of the familiar and very important Scott character, whom we first met in Waverley himself—the man
between. From now on, despite all his protestations, his
mother knows that the chords of the mind on which she is
trying to play are really there.

⁂ Encouraged by this, she tricks him into delaying his journey
so late that a punctual arrival becomes impossible. She
thinks she has conquered him, because she calculates that
his proud spirit will never consent to undergo the punishment, and therefore he will have no choice but to desert
altogether. She expects him to be angry, but when his first
anger has cooled he speaks in a way that surprises her: " 'I
have lost my all, mother, since I have broken my word, and
lost my honour.' "

This is a momentous sentence, because it introduces for
the first time into the mother's mind the notion of a debate
about fundamentals. Elspat has taken it for granted that all
her kinsmen would agree about the nature of honour. It is a
concept so deeply rooted in the clan traditions that its ambiguity has been overlooked. Now here is her son twisting its
meaning into a new form, altering honour as dignity to
honour as truth. She offers to await the soldiers coming to
arrest him and fob them off with a circumstantial story
about his death; she offers flight into wilder parts of the
Highlands, forgetting or never having realised that nowhere
now remains where the conditions which existed before 1745
still prevail. When this makes no impression on her son she
wanders off wildly, half hoping to perish on the mountains.
But growing calmer she returns to find him still uncertain
what to do. There are two courses open to him; he can make
his way back to the depot as fast as possible and endure the
punishment for outstaying his leave, or he can run away,
hide in the hills and perhaps eventually emigrate. But the
point of the story and the salient feature of the events that
follow is that he cannot choose either alternative.

We are all well accustomed in our reading of more recent literature to the indecisive intellectual hero, and to the corresponding figure in life, well-represented by Coleridge, an exact contemporary of Scott's own. We are not so familiar with the indecisive man of action, and we may even be tempted to wonder whether he is not a contradiction. But really Scott is here making a point of the highest importance. The more a man is an unreflective, passionate actor, the more he depends on the unquestioned assumptions of the society around him. The great interest of the story here is that it shows the point of breaking between two generations. The mother, having had her character formed before the break came, cannot understand her son's dilemma. It is possible to live by traditional assumptions entirely, and it is possible to form standards by personal choice. For Hamish it is too late in history to do the first, and impossible through temperament and early training to do the second. He is trying to live the old instinctive life with *two* sets of assumptions which at some points are irreconcilable. The inaction of the man of action at this moment of crisis is thus entirely in the logic of events. The struggle of principles in his mind is unfamiliar and therefore debilitating. He can only wait in agony without any clear idea of what he will do when the soldiers arrive to arrest him. The words that Scott gives him to convey to his mother this complicated state of mind are magnificent in their simplicity and economy: " 'You have taken my life; to that you have a right, for you gave it; but touch not my honour! It came to me from a brave train of ancestors . . .' " He is trying to do the impossible, to graft the new honour on to the old tradition; he cannot forget his ancestors, but neither can he imitate them or agree with them.

Even in the uncomprehending eyes of his mother he never appears as a weakling. There are moments when he reminds her irresistibly of his father; he is no weaker than his ancestors either in war or will; only he is placed under a greater strain than any of them. As he waits helplessly, he cannot even decide whether it is his intention to resist arrest, or to accept it peaceably and attempt to excuse his delay.

When the soldiers arrive, Hamish is waiting with his gun ready to fire. His mother is whispering from behind: " 'My son, beware the scourge' ". He calls to the sergeant, who had been his friend " 'I would not hurt you willingly,—but I will not be taken unless you can assure me against the Saxon lash'. "Fool!" comes the answer, "you know I cannot; yet I will do all I can. I will say I met you on your return, and the punishment will be light!"

Then Hamish fires, and Cameron falls dead. It is fitting that he should fire just after being assured that his punishment will be light. It will be light, but it will involve an intolerable affront to personal dignity. It is natural that after all uncertainties, in the final moment of crisis the hereditary standards should overcome those only partially acquired in adult life. But the reproach of one of the soldiers goes deep: " 'Are you not an accursed creature,' said one of the men to Hamish, 'to have slain your best friend, who was contriving during the whole march how he could find some way of getting you off without punishment for your desertion?'

'Do you hear *that*, mother?' said Hamish . . .' "[1]

Hamish is executed and Elspat is left in a silent solitude that is both the grey aftermath of a personal tragedy and a moving emblem of the dying Highland society so vividly pictured by Dr. Johnson.

The Two Drovers is a tauter and more exciting story with a similar theme. Two cattle-drovers, an Englishman and a Highlander who believes himself to be of noble ancestry, have a quarrel. The Englishman wants to settle it in what he

[1] *The Highland Widow* chap 5.

thinks a friendly way with his fists. When this is refused with proud contempt, he strikes the first blow and taunts his friend with cowardice. When warned that the Scotsman may take vengeance he says, with complete trust: "Robin Oig is an honest fellow, and will never keep malice." Then Robin Oig returns and kills him with a dagger, but refuses to strike again at another member of the party who has hampered him, saying, " 'It were very just to lay you beside him, but the blood of a base pickthank shall never mix on my father's dirk with that of a brave man.' " Robin then yields himself willingly to the death penalty, " 'I gave a life for the life I took, and what can I do more?' "

There is one aspect of *The Highland Widow* which receives an important new development here. We are told there that Cameron was Hamish's best friend, but the idea cannot make much impression as we have no account of their life together, and the whole action takes place near the widow's solitary cottage. But in *The Two Drovers* this mutual respect and liking is essential, and so the whole impression made by the story is surprisingly different despite the close similarity of plot. *The Highland Widow* is the story of one culture ruthlessly blotted out by another. *The Two Drovers* is the story of a failure of comprehension which is fatal in its consequences in the particular case, but only partial and perhaps not incurable. There are possibilities, however vague, of a synthesis of culture.

But, different as they are, both stories reveal with great force the closeness of the relation between a man's own inner sense of personal dignity and honour and the agreed conventions of the society in which he is educated. This inner dignity is seen as genuinely free and spontaneous; yet only society can provide the nourishment on which it thrives. We have seen in the case of Edie Ochiltree that the solitary prophetic voice is also in a way a social voice. We see in the lives of the heroes who are 'men between' like Waverley and Morton in *Old Mortality*, the strains suffered by men who find themselves involved in two different sets of social assumptions. In *The Highland Widow* we see that even a strong will and a high courage will collapse unless the foundations hold; and the foundations, for the unreflecting at least, cannot be the product of argument, cannot be derived from reason. They must be there, they must be given, they must be formed in the cradle.

The Highland Widow is the tragedy of the man for whom these foundations fail. In *The Two Drovers*, the tragic source is just the opposite. Both protagonists are strongly rooted in their own traditions. The trouble is that traditions are alike in so many ways that the crucial point of difference is not realized until it is too late. Members of cultures totally unlike might agree better than the Highlander and the Englishman, who are near enough to imagine that they mean the same thing by honesty; when they find they do not, the sense of outraged betrayal is too sudden for parleyings. The two stories taken together seem to present a crossroads with every way marked 'no thoroughfare'. To be deprived of your unquestioned assumptions leads to an inner collapse. To follow them without thought leads to bloody conflicts between one culture and another.

Very much of Scott's thinking does indeed endorse this gloomy conclusion. But the importance of the prophetic voice and of the 'man between' is that they throw a faint light on a difficult onward path. The prophetic voice of an Edie Ochiltree shows that it is possible to draw strength from the sources of a culture to criticize its actual operation. Waverley and Morton show that it is sometimes possible, though very difficult, to do what Hamish in *The Highland Widow* could not do. It is possible, if the cultures have enough originally in common, to make a synthesis, to purify for one's own use each tradition of its harsh extremities. But this cannot, for Scott, be done by simple compromise, still less by airily rejecting inherited assumptions. It can be done only by entering imaginatively into the hidden principles of each set of assumptions, and finding a reconciliation at a level far deeper than the political.

So it is that when we consider Scott's case, words like rebel and conservative tend to lose their value. It was *because* he was the most social of novelists that he gave such value to the outcast. It was because he knew so well how arbitrary and local are most of society's agreed assumptions that he insisted so constantly upon their value. For him each culture is a separate growth, and no alteration that goes deep enough to count can be achieved by arbitrary fiat. To an extraordinary extent Scott here stands outside the current debate of his time and of the generation before. All the argument between the Augustan and the devotee of the noble savage, all the cultural questions raised by Rousseau, all the arguments for liberty and against authority presented by Blake—these are not the point for Scott. I have no wish to maintain that he was a greater man than these great men. That is not a very interesting question. But he had one priceless advantage which they, weighted down and bemused by the suspect glories of French and English culture in their 'rational' phase, could not have—his position as a Border Scot with a romantic enthusiasm for Highland culture coupled with a sound legal training and a sensibility formed by the tradition of the 'rational' giants of Edinburgh: Hume and Robertson. This enabled him to undercut the conventional dichotomy, accepted each in his own way, by Rousseau, by Voltaire, by Pope, by Johnson, by Blake, between civilization and savagery, or authority and freedom. He saw that what is called savagery is only a highly organized, traditional culture seen from a particular uncomprehending point of view. Hence his great subject, eminent alike in originality and in importance is the clash of cultures and the limitations of their conventions. If we look at the matter

61

in this light, the persons of Waverley and Edie Ochiltree and the Highland widow's son all contribute something. So do the characters that represent not the flux but the solidity of culture, like Baron Bradwardine and Bailie Nicol Jarvie. Here Scott gives us something that no one else in his age can give, and no successor can give so well.

4 *Cause and Effect*

The formal principle of the realistic novel is probability. The great masters, Richardson, Jane Austen, George Eliot, even Dickens (though not always) introduce us to a situation, a set of social assumptions, and a definite time and place. They give us a deep insight into the minds of a few characters, and a general knowledge of the nature of the other characters with whom these few have to reckon. Then, they tell us what followed, and, in doing so, they issue an implied challenge to show them wrong at any point. We take up the challenge and the books we call faultless, like *Clarissa Harlowe* and *Emma*, are those where we are forced to admit that our effort has failed. Hence the course of the plot, and the coherence of personal motive and action (which in the last resort is the same thing as plot) are of the highest importance.

If this view is accepted, then the fact that a novel tells a story, far from being an embarrassing survival of primitive amusements, becomes the essential fact about it. It follows also that the *donnée*, the original characters, situations and events, become, once they have been explained in the opening chapters, *public property*. Once the idea of a given personality has emerged clearly, a novelist has forfeited the right to be trusted when he tells us that a character did or said or thought something. Now, of course, in many of the novels we read, even those with some sort of classic reputation, it is little use quarrelling with the author on these points. It is not worth exposing the deficiencies of *Tom Jones* or *The Egoist* on these scores, though it may be worth arguing in favour of their merits in other respects and judged by other standards.

It is important to remember, too, that there is a whole class of novels, including some works of remarkable quality, that do not so much fail the test as refuse to enter for it. Among these, books I particularly admire myself are nearly all the works of Peacock, some of Disraeli, and the immature works of Dickens. The assumption made here, however, is that brilliant works such as these are not and cannot be the greatest masterpieces of prose fiction; and that an irresponsible attitude to plot is a legitimate licence for the purpose of witty comment on politics, or for romantic myth, and for certain other specialized purposes, but the most central, characteristic and admirable novels take the logic of events very seriously indeed.

In making these assumptions, I am not (knowingly) wandering far from the general critical wisdom of the race. It is obvious that they are assumptions that raise particular difficulties about historical novels generally. It is my guess that these difficulties are among the strongest reasons for Scott having failed so far to attain the high classic status to which I believe his best works entitle him. The question of his use of plot, and the closely related question of historical cause as he conveys it are thus seen to be of crucial importance in deciding what, in the end, we are to think of him.

Now it is abundantly obvious that Scott is capable, at times, of being as irresponsible about plot as Peacock or Disraeli, and that when he is, he usually carries it off with much less grace and witty insolence than they do. He uses the worn paraphernalia of the eighteenth century sensational novel, and he adds on his own account the psychological naïveties of costume drama, as when Raleigh spreads his cloak for Queen Elizabeth. With all this and with his mediaevalism, I deal briefly in the next chapter. More daunting is the fact that in books of another kind, when he is at his most serious, he sometimes drops into the irresponsible manner, especially near the end. Sometimes he is himself aware of this as at the end of *Guy Mannering*; sometimes he seems to be persuading himself that he hasn't lapsed at all, or that 'it was only a little one'. Thus the faultlessness posited at the opening of this chapter is a quality that can only very seldom be accorded to Scott, and I leave the complicated question of just how near perfection his best books come to the second section of this book. For the moment, I want to focus attention on his treatment of causation at its finest, and my contention will be that it fully equals in consistency, subtlety and consequent artistic power the practice of the great masters with whose names I began the chapter. Secondly, and perhaps more important, I shall contend that his practice is original and personal to himself in introducing and mastering new types of causation, unknown to Richardson, Jane Austen, and to their great successors after Scott, and that this originality is inextricably linked with Scott's status as a historical novelist.

The issues then are wide and the critical questions at stake here momentous. But the evidence can only be clearly seen in small samples. The comparative brevity of the passages analysed below should not be allowed to conceal the general nature of the argument.

I begin with the battle of Drumclog[1].

The battle of Drumclog is an authentic example of an event which is very rare in history, the defeat in pitched battle of a brave and well-commanded force of trained soldiers by undisciplined, irregular and poorly-armed local forces. Scott responded, of course, to the romance of this; but he responded even more keenly to the intellectual problem of causation which it posed.

[1] *Old Mortality* chaps 15 and 16.

The first thing to notice is that Scott's causation does not involve 'iron laws of necessity'. Accident plays its part by allowing Claverhouse's force to come within sight of the enemy unexpectedly. The scouts have been slack, and until he actually sees the enemy Claverhouse has had no idea that they were very near. The importance of this accident is immediately magnified by two other factors. First, the insurgents, though irregulars, have in Burley and one or two others, leaders of professional training and expertise, and the nature of the ground they have chosen is very favourable to defence: "The brow of the hill, on which the royal Life-Guards were now drawn up, sloped downwards (on the side opposite to that which they had ascended) with a gentle declivity, for more than a quarter of a mile, and presented ground, which, though unequal in some places, was not altogether unfavourable for the manœuvres of cavalry, until near the bottom, when the slope terminated in a marshy level, traversed through its whole length by what seemed either a natural gully or a deep artificial drain, the sides of which were broken by springs, trenches filled with water, out of which peats and turf had been dug, and here and there by some straggling thickets of alders, which loved the moistness so well that they contined to live as bushes, although too much dwarfed by the sour soil and the stagnant bog-water to ascend into trees. Beyond this ditch or gully the ground rose into a second heathy swell, or rather hill, near to the foot of which, and as if with the object of defending the broken ground and ditch that covered their front, the body of the insurgents appeared to be drawn up with the purpose of abiding battle." Scott then describes the three lines of infantry drawn up behind this strong position, with fairly well-armed men in the first rank, and rustics with rude weapons made from farm implements in the rear, and explains how a small band of irregular cavalry guarded the firmer ground on the flanks.

While the insurgents steel their courage by the singing of a metrical psalm, Claverhouse examines the position, and concludes: "The churls must have some old soldiers among them; it was no rustic that made choice of that ground."

Such are the circumstances, in which geographical facts, tactical skill, accident and human error (by Claverhouse's scouts) are inextricably mixed, which Claverhouse and his three officers have to consider. The character and past experience of each of these four men are discernible factors in the outcome. Dick Grahame, Claverhouse's nephew, is an ordinary, brave, high-spirited upper-class boy, for whom loyalty to the King and the military traditions of his family are unquestioned assumptions. It is natural that he should confuse his class-contempt for the 'churls' opposite with the illusion that the churls would never stand against trained soldiers led by gentlemen. It is natural, too, that he should confuse his own boyish wish to prove himself in battle with the imperious, objective call of honour. Of course, he is all for immediate attack.

Major Allan is a sensible old soldier, a veteran of the Parliamentary wars, and mindful of the battle of Dunbar nearly thirty years before. His is the veteran's unselfconscious courage; he believes in being brave in order to win victories, not in order to prove that one is brave. Moreover, he knows that there is more than one conception of military honour in the world, and that the Covenanters, like Cromwell's armies in the past, have an inspiration different from his own but just as capable of fostering endurance in battle. He sees, too, what Grahame chooses to neglect, "These fellows are three or four to one—I should not mind that much upon a fair field, but they are posted in a very formidable strength [i.e. of position, not numbers], and show no inclination to quit it."

As the old man and the young begin to squabble about

their different conceptions of courage, Claverhouse breaks in, and his wider and more intelligent grasp of the political implications of war paradoxically leads him to agree with the hot-headed cornet rather than with the shrewd major. He sees that Major Allan's correct tactical advice cannot be accepted, because in war morale is everything, and the news of a retreat of royal troops in the face of irregular forces would sway all the waverers of the Lowlands to the opposing side. (Here, of course, lies the great importance of the 'rascally scouts'. Given proper information, Claverhouse could have avoided contact with the enemy at this time without loss of face.)

It is worth noting as characteristic of Scott's method when his powerful intelligence is really working that there is a certain ample casualness about his presentation of its fruits. Of the few other novelists capable of comprehending and presenting such a paradox, most would have been detected hugging themselves and pointing out their cleverness to the reader.

But now a fourth, and very different note is heard. Lord Evandale is one of those soldiers, brave and dutiful as others, who nevertheless reject the conventional belief in the glories of war. He speaks, to the surprise and annoyance of Claverhouse, of the enemy as 'misguided men' and 'Scotchmen and subjects of King Charles', and he proposes a parley and the offer to the enemy that they may disperse with a free pardon. But Claverhouse, again, though narrower and harsher in his party spirit, is yet more perceptive about political realities. "Their leaders" he says with truth, "who have all been most active in the murder of the Archbishop of St. Andrews, fight with a rope round their necks, and are likely to kill the messenger, were it but to dip their followers in loyal blood, and to make them as desperate of pardon as themselves."

Now that the grim prospect for any bearer of the message

he advocates is pointed out to him, Evandale has no choice but to volunteer for the office himself. He has no choice, but he also does it with spontaneous courage. Claverhouse, however, prefers to send his own nephew as a man of less weight in society and therefore more expendable, while the prospect of ordering his own heir to do something that will probably lead to his immediate death perhaps appeals to his own pride in his grim stoic courage. Here again is a paradox. The logic of events and the personal nature of the three men means that Grahame will necessarily be the one chosen to carry out the policy to which he most of all is opposed, and he cannot hesitate for a moment, because the most pacific policy is also the most dangerous for him personally, and therefore at this moment makes the strongest appeal to his warlike instincts.

Grahame rides forward with a white flag and all happens as Claverhouse had so shrewdly foreseen. Burley sees a grand opportunity to ensure a decision by force of arms, since a truce would be bound to exclude him as a murderer of the Archbishop. Thus, for him, a truce is much more dangerous than war. He kills Grahame, and so small is the geographical scale of all these events that the royalist officers can see him fall. This makes a battle inevitable, and, as we have seen, the odds are all against the royal forces. But it does more, for the sight of Grahame's fall, shocking to them all, is peculiarly terrible to Evandale, who suggested the plan and feels that he himself should have borne the flag. It is illogical, but perfectly natural that he should experience the emotion of shame felt by a man who has sent another to die in his place. Naturally, too, his sense of military discipline and order will be overborne by this powerful feeling that he must at once blot out this shame by a personal act of reckless courage. And so he charges forward at once at the head of his own men and those of Grahame, too, for now there are only two officers left subordinate to the commander. And so, the last chance of victory, which lies in a disciplined and even advance, is lost.

What Scott has done here in a scene of incomparable penetration, vividness and economy is to cut the sterile knot of argument about material and personal factors in history. By comparison with this, Carlyle's hero-worship, salted with vague ineluctable forces of destiny, and the later naïveties of political historicism seem crude indeed.

But, it might be said, Scott's analysis here, brilliant though it is, deals solely with an event of comparative unimportance. There is a wider stream of causation that leads to Bothwell Brig, where the victory of the royal forces more than cancelled the effect of Drumclog, and a wider yet, with its sources outside Scotland, that will lead in a few more years to the failure of the present royal policy. Scott does not here have much to say about the last, though he had already shown in *Waverley* that he could deal brilliantly also with the widest social tendencies. Perhaps it would have been a mistake to try to include every magnitude of events in a single narrative. But he is not satisfied until he has put a set-piece like Drumclog into perspective.

He achieves this here by showing the spirit and predicament of the irregular army when they realize the extent of their victory. "Their success seemed even to have upon their spirits the effect of a sudden and violent surprise, so much had their taking up arms been a measure of desperation rather than of hope. Their meeting was also casual, and they had hastily arranged themselves under such commanders as were remarkable for zeal and courage, without much respect to any other qualities. It followed from this state of disorganization that the whole army appeared at once to resolve itself into a general committee for considering what steps were to be taken in consequence of their success, and no opinion could be started so wild that it had not some favourers and advocates. Some proposed that they should march to Glasgow, some to Hamilton, some to Edinburgh, some to London. Some were for sending a deputation of their number to London to convert Charles II to a sense of the error of his ways; and others, less charitable, proposed either to call a new successor to the crown, or to declare Scotland a free republic. A free parliament of the nation, and a free assembly of the Kirk, were the objects of the more sensible and moderate of the party. In the meanwhile a clamour arose among the soldiers for bread and other necessaries, and while all complained of hardship and hunger, none took the necessary measures to secure supplies. In short, the camp of the Covenanters, even in the very moment of success, seemed about to dissolve like a rope of sand, from want of the original principles of combination and union."[1]

How brilliantly and unobtrusively the aims and methods of the novelist and the historian are interwoven. Scott has no need here of a historical analysis because he is able as a simple storyteller describing what people did and thought to imply all that a longer historical digression could give. The economic difficulties, the effect of lack of discipline, the incompatibility of aims among the leaders are all there. But there is something more, something which is always for the real historian among his most intractable problems. How to get things in proportion? We have just seen Drumclog as it appeared in the intensity of experience to the participants on the day. We are in no danger of forgetting that such an event in human terms is great because the deepest impulses are at work and the deepest feelings are stirred. We now have to move back as students of history to see the (comparatively small) significance of the event in a whole international conflict. Scott can show us this without commenting himself because he has only to show the disproportion between what

---

[1] *Old Mortality* chap 18.

the participants felt they had achieved and what they had really achieved. 'To convert Charles II, to declare a new king or a republic,'—as soon as these aims are mentioned we see the incongruity, and our mental scale changes to the international level.[1]

But it is characteristic of the geniality of Scott's method that this does not quite have the effect of a cold douche. All the materials are here for one of those disturbing changes of scale that occur in the transitions of *Gulliver's Travels*. But the actual experience of reading here is quite different. There is no call for the reader to feel tricked. The high heroic emotions, and the delicate analysis of causes to which he responded as he read the account of Drumclog are as valid as ever. For Scott one kind of experience cannot refute another; the aim is rather a more comprehensive view that will grasp the main pattern and the significant detail at the same time. Here perhaps, above all, is the value to Scott as a historical novelist of his wide and deep erudition. True, it could at times lead him astray into irrelevant displays of expertise about heraldry or armour. But the dullness of these passages, which occur most often in the books set in ages furthest from his own, is a small price to pay for the balance and proportion which erudition helped him to find in his accounts of the social changes of the seventeenth and eighteenth centuries. To know the order of magnitude of each of the

---

[1] Sometimes the transposition into another scale has wider connotations still, suggesting not merely wider public issues, but a comparison with forces more than human. For instance: "The power of man at no time appears more contemptible than when placed in contrast with scenes of natural terror and dignity. The victorious army of Montrose, *whose exploits had struck terror into all Scotland*, when ascending up this terrific pass, seemed a contemptible handful of stragglers, *in the act of being devoured by the jaws of the mountain*, which appeared ready to close upon them." (*A Legend of Montrose* chapter 17. My italics.)

historical events with which he dealt had become second nature. He is able to get it right in the style of a learned man talking at ease, allusively, rather than in the style of a lecturer.

The detailed treatment given to this one example makes it superfluous, I hope, to analyse any similar cases. But of many passages which would yield a similar impression of Scott's masterly originality in the treatment of causation, the Porteous riots in *The Heart of Midlothian* might be mentioned, or, in somewhat simpler vein, the mixed military and political calculations of the regent Murray at the end of *The Monastery*.

But Scott sometimes employed an entirely different method, and started, as it were, at the other end. Then, instead of building up events out of their basic causes, he showed the telescoped effect in a single scene of one of the great turning points of history. A good example can be found in the early chapters of *Peveril of the Peak*, and especially chapter 7.

The protagonists, Sir Geoffrey Peveril and Major Bridgenorth, one a zealous royalist, the other a Presbyterian, and former officer in Cromwell's army, are each in different ways puzzled by the Restoration of Charles II, and the rapid events of the year 1660. For Peveril it is, of course, the consummation always wished for; Bridgenorth gives, as Presbyterians generally did, a reluctant consent for fear of army rule or fresh revolution. Each is in his way a man of good will; they are country neighbours, and bound together by old memories and by family ties. They want and need to be friends, and like the country at large they are sick of strife and uncertainty. So Peveril arranges a grand celebration at which the tenants, followers and servants of Bridgenorth and himself will drown all discord. When the Bridgenorth faction revive their drooping spirits with memories of old victories in battle and with singing of the metrical psalms, they rouse uneasy memories in the minds of the former cavaliers.

" 'Adad,' said the old knight' [Sir Jasper Cranbourne], 'may I never taste claret again, if that is not the very tune with which the prick-eared villains began their onset at Wiggan Lane, when they trowled us down like so many ninepins! Faith, neighbours, to say truth and shame the devil, I did not like the sound of it above half.'

'If I thought the Roundheaded rogues did it in scorn of us,' said Dick Wildblood of the Dale, 'I would cudgel their psalmody out of their peasantly throats with this very truncheon. . . .'

' We'll have no ranting, Dick,' said the old knight to the young franklin—'adad, man, we'll have none, for three reasons: first because it would be ungentle to Lady Peveril; then, because it is against the king's peace; and lastly, Dick, because, if we did set on the psalm-singing knaves, thou mightest come by the worst, my boy, as has chanced to thee before.'[1]

After this the celebration passes off with some awkwardness and embarrassment, but peacefully. Everyone can feel he has performed a difficult duty and that the first and most arduous period of reconciliation is over. But Sir Jasper's casual phrase, 'the king's peace' contains, potentially, a puzzling dilemma, and what follows makes this dilemma crucial.

The Countess of Derby is a more irreconcilable royalist partisan than Peveril and Cranbourne, she is an old friend of the Peveril family, and the widow and mother of men traditionally accustomed to exercise quasi-royal authority in the Isle of Man. She admits, or rather states (for she is in no way ashamed) that she has had one Edward Christian executed as a traitor. Bridgenorth overhears, and his political

---

[1] *Peveril of the Peak* chap 4.

views and his personal connection with Christian's family
alike encourage him to regard this 'execution' as a case of
murder. He goes away and reappears with a party of officers
of the peace, and a royal warrant for the Countess of Derby's
arrest.

" 'Sir Geoffrey,' said the major, 'I have no time for jesting:
I am on the King's affairs.'

'Are you sure it is not upon Old Noll's, neighbour? You
used to hold his the better errand,' said the knight, with a
smile which gave occasion to a horse-laugh among his
followers.

'Show him your warrant,' said Bridgenorth to the man in
black formerly mentioned, who was a pursuivant. Then
taking the warrant he gave it Sir Geoffrey. 'To this at least,
you will pay regard.'

"The same regard which you would have paid it a month
back or so', said the knight, tearing the warrant to shreds.
'What a plague do you stare at? Do you think you have a
monopoly of rebellion, and that we have not a right to show
a trick of disobedience in our turn?'

'Make way, Sir Geoffrey Peveril,' said Bridgenorth, 'or
you will compel me to do that I may be sorry for. I am in
this matter the avenger of the blood of one of the Lord's
saints, and I will follow the chase while Heaven grants me
an arm to make my way.'

'You shall make no way here but at your peril', said Sir
Geoffrey; 'this is my ground. I have been harassed enough
these twenty years by saints, as you call yourselves. I tell you,
master, you shall neither violate the security of my house,
nor pursue my friends over the grounds, nor tamper, as you
have done, amongst my servants, with impunity. I have had
you in respect for certain kind doings, which I will not
either forget or deny, and you will find it difficult to make
me draw a sword or bend a pistol against you. . . . And for
these rascals, who come hither to annoy a noble lady on my

75

bounds, unless you draw them off, I will presently send some of them to the devil before their time.' "[1]

There follows a scuffle, but no bloodshed. Bridgenorth prudently drops his plan of enforcing the warrant. The matter is remitted to the Government with Clarendon at its head, and eventually a heavy fine is substituted for the capital charge.

With what economy and dramatic simplicity Scott has here presented the actual working in the actions of simple men of the complicated legal and constitutional issues which arise after a counter-revolution. How natural is Sir Geoffrey's inability to see the difference between resistance to the operation of the law in criminal causes and a politico-military resistance to the exercise of royal power. How incongruous and yet how logical is Bridgenorth's attempt to vindicate the blood of the saints by the authority of him whom a year or two before he would no doubt have described as an infidel, papistical whoremaster, and worthy son of the accursed persecutor of the saints, Charles I. How natural it is that Peveril should be slow to comprehend what Bridgenorth seizes avidly upon, that the royalists of the Civil War, in attaining their object in the King's restoration, must inevitably renounce something else. They must give up their private ownership, as it were, of the King as their own party-leader and rallying-cry. The logic of their own argument, as well as the logic of events, requires the royalists eventually to admit that the King is now the king of all the people, the keeper of the peace and the enforcer of the law. Murder must now be a civil crime not a party question. In passages like this Scott, as no one before, and few since, found the point of intersection between great historical events and the local interests, everyday concerns and personal passions of ordinary men. If the theorists of causation seem naïve in the

[1] *ibid* chap 7.

face of Scott's masterly account of Drumclog, here the pur-
veyors of 'everyday life' as the stuff of history are put to
shame. The daily routine of simple people presented as the
stuff of history is inadequate because of its lack of context,
its neglect of the power of ideas and traditions in human
affairs. But simple people do not consciously formulate
difficult ideas. The dilemma appears inescapable until Scott
shows the way out, and convinces us that unreflective men
like Peveril and Bridgenorth are implicitly acting upon or
are thwarted by the working of complex political and legal
concepts. The later part of *Peveril of the Peak* is not worthy of
this fine opening, but the actual achievement here is of a
high order. It is hard to imagine a more difficult feat than
the resolution of broad historical changes into their practical
equivalents in the lives of particular men.

We have seen then how Scott could master the subtle
tissue of causes in a single event, and reveal the multiple
reflections of a major historical event such as the Restoration
in the lives of ordinary men. The third achievement is in
some ways the most important of all, but does not lend itself
to the same exactness of analysis. In the widest historical
perspective, in the whole manner of thinking of past periods,
Scott found his eighteenth century predecessors much at
fault. Everyone must have been struck with the fact that the
great writers of the eighteenth century, Pope and Gibbon,
for instance, are curiously self-contradictory when they apply
their general view of human nature to the past. They always
speak as if human nature was everywhere the same. But
then they dismiss whole periods of history as beneath contempt, with phrases like 'monkish ignorance' and 'barbarism
and religion'. Scott saw that the weakness of this approach
was that it was in one sense too social and in another not
social enough. It was too social in the sense that it attached
too absolute and general a value to a particular social ideal,
and the personal moral standards required by a given society.

77

(The actual society chosen might be the age of Augustus or the Antonines, or the France of Louis XIV or eighteenth century England.) It was not social enough in the sense that it underrated the practical influence of education and environment in a given society upon personal character. When this is understood the paradox by which Gibbon and Pope implied that human nature was everywhere the same, but that some human societies were worth taking seriously and some were not, suddenly becomes intelligible. They could not comprehend the particularity of the social influences that helped to form both themselves and the men they most admired, because they implicitly regarded Augustan standards as generally valid. Thus they felt able to dismiss the wide deviations from these that they encountered in the study of the history or literature of the past as barbarous. The idea that there could be high civilizations of contrasting kinds, and on irreconcilable principles, was grasped vaguely and intermittently, if at all.

A very interesting partial exception to this is Dr. Johnson. Scott could have learnt a lot from *A Journey to the Western Islands*. (I cannot find much evidence that he actually did so.) For there Johnson in a most original way shows the deadly impact of one civilization on another, shows the inevitable triumph of the commercial, Hanoverian spirit on a venerable and defeated society. He shows too, though only in brief sketches, something of the dilemmas and strains imposed on those who live between two worlds. Johnson was able to do this because he saw for himself the visible remains of past history, and because he could reason so keenly from appearance to probable past fact, and also because of his sympathy with an older religious tradition. Thus accounts of barbarous mass vengeance performed by the Highland clans, or of exceedingly primitive economic arrangements are balanced by contrary passages like this from the description of Raasay:

"It has been, for many years, popular to talk of the lazy devotion of the Romish clergy; over the sleepy laziness of men that erected churches, we may indulge our superiority with a new triumph by comparing it with the fervid activity of those who suffer them to fall." Johnson marks a step away from the abstract human nature of Pope, of Hume, maintained also by his junior, Gibbon, in his awareness of the importance of material factors. He has a most acute analysis of the influence of mountainous terrain on local culture, and always reveals the keenest curiosity about methods of agriculture, building and travel. But in its extraordinary intelligence and originality, though not in its humane sympathy, The *Journey* remains something of an exception among Johnson's works. Or rather, for I am far from wishing to suggest that Johnson was ever other than highly intelligent, he did not habitually turn his mind to problems of this sort and the historical mode of thought was not his métier.

Scott shared with Johnson this salutary low-mindedness, which allowed both to give full weight to material factors in history. But for our purpose he had two great advantages that Johnson lacked. He had really wide historical knowledge and interest, and thus the opportunity for wider-ranging and more exact comparisons. And, writing after the French Revolution, he found it much easier than Johnson did to detach himself from the endemic illusion that one particular phase of human civilization had attained an exclusive classic status. Johnson achieved this in *The Journey* but not easily, and not habitually. Thus, *The Lives of the Poets*, supremely great in its penetration of the character and motives of individuals, is comparatively dull and conventional in its treatment of the fascinating question of the relation of Augustan literature to the work of earlier writers.

Thus Scott was able to show for all to see that no human society was really formed on principles of reason, and that every clash of hostile cultures revealed each side as passion-

79

ate, unreasonable, and each form of culture as temporary. There is no final term in Scott's historical process. He is emancipated both from the revolutionary myth of progress and the Augustan myth of finality. In later chapters, especially those devoted to *Waverley, Old Mortality* and *Redgauntlet,* I attempt to show in detail how this imaginative freedom benefited his work.

Scott was fond in his books set in the seventeenth and eighteenth centuries of shifting the time by about a generation. Thus *Old Mortality* is set in 1679, *Rob Roy* in 1715, *The Heart of Midlothian* in 1736, *Redgauntlet* in about 1770, and *The Antiquary* near the turn of the century, in the days of Scott's own manhood. This enables him to show, in a way that only the imperceptive could thereafter ignore, that a given psychological type is different in different circumstances. The active fanaticism of Balfour of Burley will develop into the pessimistic stoic endurance of David Deans. The unselfconscious Highland traditionalism of Rob Roy will become another thing when in the person of Fergus Mac-Ivor it has had time to receive an admixture of French cynicism. The mean, commercial spirit of Morton's uncle in *Old Mortality* is an alien in the old, heroic world; but it will come into its own a generation later in the person of Bailie Nicol Jarvie. The efficient ruthlessness of Grahame of Claverhouse, touched already with a well-disciplined romanticism, will be transposed, three whole generations later, into Redgauntlet's matchless devotion to defeat and despair. For Scott the whole class system is in a state of change throughout the seventeenth and eighteenth centuries; seeing this is one of his most unaugustan insights.

Unaugustan, too, is his grasp of the irrational as an analysable factor in human affairs. He had, of course, the tradition of the Gothic novel behind him, and he had read the Gothic novels with care, and written essays about several of the authors. But the difference is clear and important.

80

The Castle of Otranto does not take the irrational seriously; *The Bride of Lammermoor* does. Scott saw that if the feelings and actions that spring from superstition are portrayed with sufficient force, the whole question of the objective truth or falsehood of preternatural appearances becomes, for artistic purposes, secondary.

To those who are already familiar with Scott's two main styles, the logical narrative of history, as in *Waverley*, and the fantastic romance, as in *Ivanhoe*, *The Bride of Lammermoor* is likely to be a puzzling book. For it can be read in two ways that are difficult to harmonize. Read in one way, it is a perfectly clear account of a chapter of social history. It shows how both the virtues and the vices of an aristocratic family tend towards their defeat by an ambitious politician; and the final catastrophe, violent though it is, follows naturally from facts that cannot be called improbable: the love of Edgar Ravenswood and Lucy Ashton, and the *folie de grandeur* of Lucy's mother. But in actually reading the story one is constantly distracted from this sombre and simple line of intelligible events by sibyls muttering dark prophecies, by wells to which strange legends attach, and by scraps of verse that prefigure the story. Take for instance the situation described in the third chapter. Ashton, now Lord Keeper, has possessed himself of the castle of the Ravenswood family, leaving the family's present representative with only the ruined Wolf's Crag. Edgar Ravenswood has put himself in the wrong with Government by allowing a political demonstration at his father's funeral. Ashton, anxious to make his gains at the expense of the Ravenswood family safe for the future, reflects: "Young Ravenswood is now mine—he is my own—he has placed himself in my hand, and he shall bend or break." While writing his report for the Privy Council, which is designed to ensure the punishment of Ravenswood for the late uproar without too obviously accusing him, he happens to look up, and sees the crest of the

Ravenswood family, traditional owners of the house now his own. Scott goes on:

"It was a black bull's head, with the legend, 'I bide my time'; and the occasion upon which it was adopted mingled itself singularly and impressively with the subject of his present reflections.

It was said by a constant tradition, that a Malisius de Ravenswood had, in the thirteenth century, been deprived of his castle and lands by a powerful usurper, who had for a while enjoyed his spoils in quiet. At length, on the eve of a costly banquet, Ravenswood, who had watched his opportunity, introduced himself into the castle with a small band of faithful retainers. The serving of the expected feast was impatiently looked for by the guests, and clamorously demanded by the temporary master of the castle. Ravenswood, who had assumed the disguise of a sewer upon the occasion, answered, in a stern voice, 'I bide my time'; and at the same moment a bull's head, the ancient symbol of death, was placed upon the table. The explosion of the conspiracy took place upon the signal, and the usurper and his followers were put to death. Perhaps there was something in this still known and often repeated story, which came immediately home to the breast and conscience of the Lord Keeper . . ."[1] and the upshot is that he reconsiders his report, and eventually sends one much less damaging to young Ravenswood.

So far, it is obvious, we are dealing with perfectly real psychological influences. Ashton is a cautious man, who never needs much to influence him in the direction of safety and discretion. There is nothing improbable in his heeding the warning given by such a tradition. We notice too that this passage appears to make a prediction which is not afterwards fulfilled. Almost anyone, reading the passage for the

---

[1] *The Bride of Lammermoor* chap 3.

first time, would suppose that the story would finally lead to a similar situation in which the ancient family triumphed over the newcomer. In fact, it is Edgar Ravenswood who will perish without an heir, while the power of the Ashtons flourishes. (It is true that other prophecies are made which are strangely fulfilled, but I defer consideration of these for a moment.)

But it is particularly important to notice what follows immediately after Ashton's chance look at the Ravenswood crest. First, we are introduced to his daughter, Lucy, and told of her dreamy, unpractical character, which is sure to make trouble for parents planning an ambitious marriage. She takes her father to visit the blind old woman, Alice, who has long known the Ravenswood family and warns Ashton of their future vengeance. Then they are frightened by an actual bull, whose attack is cut short by an arrow fired by Edgar Ravenswood. This happens just by a fountain, to which another ancient story of the Ravenswood family is attached. ("All agreed that the spot was fatal to the Ravenswood family.") So arises the first meeting between Edgar Ravenswood and his hereditary enemy, and the first meeting with the girl whose love will be fatal to both. Edgar Ravenswood haughtily refuses the gratitude that is his due, and leaves them with the words: 'I leave you, madam . . . to the protection of those to whom it is possible you may have this day been a guardian angel.'

These words read oddly like the key to an allegory. The threatening bull, since we have just been told of its heraldic significance as emblem of the Ravenswood family, can only be interpreted as Edgar Ravenswood threatened revenge. Revenge is checked by incipient love for the daughter, which is the point of the haughty farewell remark just quoted. Even the arrow is allegorically appropriate because of the association with Cupid.

When one has seen all this, as one cannot fail to do, the

greatest puzzle only becomes more confusing. All this sounds like Hawthorne, not Scott. Since when did Scott write allegory? And if, exceptionally, he did so here, why should he want to when his story is realistic and its progression logical, when his usual grasp of class questions and economic influences is as firm as ever?

The answer to these difficult questions becomes somewhat easier if we turn to some of the book's later prophecies, and in particular the strange verse summary of the story's end:

> When the last Laird of Ravenswood
>   to Ravenswood shall ride,
> And woo a dead maiden to be his bride,
> He shall stable his steed in the Kelpie's flow,
> And his name shall be lost for evermore!

Every item of this prophecy is exactly fulfilled, but it is presented as an old rhyme known by Caleb Balderstone and recited by him to Edgar Ravenswood. Now I think I am right in saying that many readers are aware of curiously mixed feelings about this prophecy and its neat fulfilment. Our ordinary everyday mind, including the ordinary critical mind, rejects them as melodramatic, and (more important) as detracting from the suspense and the human significance of the story's climax. Yet this apparently very reasonable judgment is not felt (by me, at any rate) to be fully satisfactory. Not only are the lines haunting and memorable in themselves, but they do not seem to spoil the exciting story that follows.

Nor is the story spoilt, as we might expect it would be by a recurrence nearer the climax of the semi-allegorical mode. In chapter 20, Edgar Ravenswood and Lucy Ashton are talking together as lovers in the wood, when a raven is shot by Lucy's brother near enough to spatter her clothes with blood. This, of course, prefigures the blood-feud of the two families, and the death of Lucy, while the punning coincidence of raven-in-the-wood and the name Ravenswood might be felt tiresome, and is certainly facile.

If all these objections, which seem on the face of it very sensible, do not really answer with accuracy to our actual literary experience in reading *The Bride of Lammermoor*, why is this? I suggest the following answer. Scott was not really writing about prophecies and the preternatural at all. Still less was he writing allegory. He was writing with great intelligence and control about the relation between fact and legend. But instead of analysing the difference as most people would do in a like case, he places the fact and the legend side by side at every point in the story. The haunting rhyme just quoted is what the folk consciousness would naturally make up afterwards about the later events of the book. By allowing it to be invented before as a prophecy, Scott shows the way the legendary mind actually works. He shows the real process of the formation of myth. He shows at every point the reality behind the myth, the class-struggle, the proud resentment of a dispossessed aristocrat, the practical influence of omens on conduct, the real experience of living in a superstitious society. By this method superstition is humanized, legend is shown to be relevant to the deepest concerns of the society that produces it. The real logic of events is there, but also there is the indisputable fact that people seldom realize the logic of events in their own lives, least of all when they are keyed up to intense emotions. When it is all over, we say, "I always said it would be so". Instead of dissecting the untruth of this Scott shows us what it is like to come to believe it. He gives us the sense of fate not as a reality but as a universal conviction of the men of a given society, and he shows that this belief like all fundamental beliefs about the nature of life has real effects. The fatalism of the characters is an intelligible element of the story.[1]

[1] The effectiveness of this method in *The Bride of Lammermoor*

It is a strange and unusual method. But when we understand it we shall see both that it is very characteristic of Scott and that it has great advantages, from a literary point of view, over eighteenth century rationalism. It is characteristic of Scott because he did not need to believe in the supernatural to find it imaginatively real and satisfying. Its advantages over the Voltairean and Gibbonian approach are by now, I hope, obvious. Scott reveals to us the actual experience of living in a society where rational causes are little considered and where omen, prophecy, presentiment are taken seriously. 'Nihil humanum alienum puto'. The Augustans may have believed this, but in their treatment of legend and superstitition, they did not act on it. Scott did, because he felt the imaginative power of the legends himself, though he believed them perhaps as little as Gibbon believed in miracles.

But one must not press this too far. Nineteenth century literature after Scott, from Keats to Rossetti and Oscar Wilde, is full of the loving treatment of legends and superstitions. Most of these literary legends appear, by the side of

---

depends, of course, on not being explicit about the method used, on *using* the method rather than on speaking of it. But that Scott was at other times consciously aware of the issue raised here can be seen from the following passage: "All the Highlands ring with prophecy that when there should be a deaf Caberfae the clan and chief shall all go to wreck, but these predictions are very apt to be framed after the event." (*Letters* vol IV p22, dated 21 January 1815.)

Similarly in chapter 8 of *Castle Dangerous* we find this: " 'No doubt,' replied the archer, with a sort of dry, civil sneer of incredulity, 'I have seldom known an insurrection in Scotland but that it was prophesied by some old, forgotten rhyme, conjured out of dust and cobwebs, for the sake of giving courage to those North Country rebels who durst not otherwise have abidden the whistling of the grey-goose shaft.' "

The Bride of Lammermoor, archaic, faded, decorative. The contrast is due to the absence, in most of the successors, of anything corresponding to the other side of Scott's mind. For Scott, here, just as much as in the battle of Drumclog, really wanted to know the truth. Thus, as we have seen, the social and psychological factors are analysed with perfect accuracy. But myths and legends are part of this psychological reality which Scott treated with respect and Gibbon with contempt.

But, as ever, Scott saw more than one side to the question. What about the dark side of superstition? What about its debilitating effect on courage and on clear thought about the causes of things? *The Pirate* stands in approximately the same relation to *The Bride* that *Rob Roy* has to *Waverley*. In *Waverley* the romance and spirit of the Jacobite cause, in *The Bride* the psychology of omen and superstition are mingled inextricably with the main action of the story. *Rob Roy* and *The Pirate* are more analytical, and each shows the weaker side of the impulses that lead to Jacobitism or to superstition.

In *The Pirate*, the cardinal distinction necessary for the whole study of Scott, between intellectual acceptance of the truth of folk-traditions and emotional involvement with them is made explicit. Of the two sister-heroines, one is a believer in the preternatural, but is not at all frightened of its manifestations, while the other is frightened but does not believe. This distinction, which seems to me entirely right, would have been barely intelligible to some of Scott's distinguished Augustan predecessors. *The Pirate* is pervaded, as *The Bride* is not, with reflective passages in which superstition is placed under the microscope of the historian, and the reader's personal involvement with the feelings of the characters becomes very faint or disappears:

"The Udaller's respect for his country extended to its superstitions, and so did the interest which he took in his unfortunate kinswoman. If he never rendered a precise assent to her high supernatural pretensions, he was not in the least desirous of hearing them disputed by others."[1] This cool, mildly sympathetic approach is here the author's also, and may well be the reader's.

At times the influences leading to superstition are shown without any of the romantic colouring thrown over them in *The Bride*:

"Indeed the scene [of the kirk of St. Ringan] was rendered more appalling to weak and ignorant minds because the same stormy and eddying winds, which, on the one side of the church, threatened to bury the ruins with sand, and had, in fact, heaped it up in huge quantities, so as almost to hide the side wall with its buttresses, seemed in other places bent on uncovering the graves of those who had been laid to their long rest on the south-eastern quarter; and, after an unusually hard gale, the coffins, and sometimes the very corpses of those who had been interred without the usual cerements, were discovered, in a ghastly manner, to the eyes of the living."[2]

In these circumstances, we can hardly be surprised at the fishermen's custom of dropping silver coins through the ruined windows to placate the forces behind the perils of the sea, and then retiring without looking behind, "for it was believed that the skeleton of the saint received the offering in his bony hand, and showed his ghastly death's-head at the window." We cannot be surprised but nor can we treat the custom as anything more than a survival. At times, indeed, Scott comes as near to the frankly rationalistic as he came to the romantic-mythical in the more extravagant passages of *The Bride*: "Here and there an old sibyl displayed the superior importance of her experience by predicting, from the appearance of the atmosphere, that the wind would

---

[1] *The Pirate* chap 21.   [2] *ibid* chap 25.

be fair or foul . . ." (chapter 20). Though the tone is mild, this is substantially what Swift or Voltaire would have seen, a shrewd weather forecast pretending to be a prophecy possessed of supernatural authority.

This chapter has not aimed to give a balanced picture of Scott's strength and weakness, but to show the range and variety of the strong points. But each example that has been analysed in some detail could, of course, be paralleled by others. The prevailing impression, for me, is of a mind of extraordinary intelligence, curiosity and force.

5 *Mediaevalist and Entertainer*

If Scott was a great artist, as it is the purpose of this book to maintain, it is obvious that he was many other things too. Without any attempt at completeness this chapter is intended to sketch some of the main tendencies in his secondary or inferior work. One of the reasons for the prevailing uncertainty about his position in our literature is that this secondary work is about two-thirds of the whole. In general, the books written after 1820 are inferior, and the books describing life more than two centuries before his own time are inferior, and these two categories tend to overlap. Clearly there are exceptions, especially in the first category, and of these *Redgauntlet* and *The Highland Widow* are notable. At the same time several of the books dealing with early times have passages of merit, or interesting ideas treated with partial success. And yet the general impression of inferiority is unmistakable, and its causes are clear. Scott was tired, and he was writing much too fast. Though a learned man in his own way, he did not know enough to recreate the earlier centuries. Moreover, he was writing for a public ready to be entertained and bewitched by an unreal middle age, a public that had emancipated itself from the stock Augustan prejudices about mediaeval barbarism, and was now ready to adopt different misconceptions, and to be deceived in new ways.

All this means that this chapter is in some ways a melancholy one for an admirer of Scott to write. But not altogether so. Scott can be dull; he can be hasty and careless. He is never cruel or self-pitying. He never fails in that fundamental respect for human life in all its forms without which literature descends to triviality. Scott at his worst is a great artist and a great man making a botch; he is never causing us to doubt whether we were mistaken after all, in reading his best books, in supposing that he was a great artist and a great man.

The historical novel depends on a synthesis of likeness and unlikeness between the time of writing and the time portrayed. If the past is presented as the present in disguise, we get the 'costume novel', and this is probably the commonest kind of failure in the tradition of historical fiction. If the past is shown as absolutely unlike the present, so that the men of the past seem to have become a different species from men as we know them, we get the Gothic novel. But in this second case, since an author can only in the end write out of his own humanity, what really happens is that a certain suppressed or despised area of the mind is allowed free play as a kind of holiday. *Romola* may serve as an example of the first kind, and *The Castle of Otranto* of the second. Scott often in his inferior works veers towards the first error, though seldom for the whole duration of a book. His inexhaustible human sympathy, his honesty, his large acceptance of himself with all his impulses and imperfections, prevented him from ever falling into the second. He is capable of making a mediaeval Jewess talk like an eighteenth century bluestocking. He is not capable, as Mrs. Radcliffe was, of making anyone talk like an abstraction of the fiendish or animal tendencies of the human mind.

There is no sense of escape in Scott's mediaevalism; and it is this, above all, that distinguishes it from so much of the mediaevalism of his century, from Keats to Rossetti. Scott had no desire to escape from anything; he had an inexhaustible curiosity about human life in all times and places. Some-

times he was well-informed and showed a profound understanding. Sometimes as in *The Abbot* he had considerable
knowledge, but an imperfect understanding. Sometimes, as
in dealing with the Saracens in *The Talisman*, his knowledge
was slight and his attempt to understand perfunctory. But
this is no more than the inevitable unevenness of grasp of a
man of extraordinary breadth of interests and ferocious
energy who composed with great rapidity. He would have
been wiser not to attempt the subject of *The Talisman*, but
he did himself no real discredit by the attempt.

The absence of that desire to escape, so strong both in his
'Gothic' predecessors and his pre-Raphaelite successors has
some surprising consequences. There is a strong strain of
worldly shrewdness, for instance, in *Quentin Durward*. Dealing with the fifteenth century, the book is able to show
chivalric customs in decline, and men repeating by force of
habit principles that are no longer the motives of conduct.
Moreover the ingenuous Scots hero is viewed with a satirical
eye. He is unable to distinguish clearly between appearance
and reality. He is influenced by the trappings of power and
the flounces of beauty. Thus Quentin meets Louis XI before
he knows who he is. When the identity is revealed: "Those
eyes, which, according to Quentin's former impression, only
twinkled with the love of gain, had, now that they were
known to be the property of an able and powerful monarch,
a piercing and majestic glance; and those wrinkles on the
brow, which he had supposed were formed during a long
series of petty schemes of commerce, seemed now the fur-
rows which sagacity had worn while toiling in meditation
upon the fate of nations."[1] Needless to say, he had been
more nearly right the first time. His feeling for rank affects
his sense of feminine charm also: "Invested now with all the
mysterious dignity belonging to the nymph of the veil and

[1] *Quentin Durward* chap 8.

lute, and proved, besides, at least in Quentin's estimation, to be the high-born heiress of a rich earldom, her beauty made ten times the impression upon him which it had done when he beheld in her one whom he deemed the daughter of a paltry innkeeper, in attendance upon a rich burgher." [1]

Uncertainties and self-deceptions like these make Quentin a suitable hero for a story in which Scott is trying to present a changing society, which has been unable to develop new theories to support its new practice, and consequently is not sure itself how much or how fast it is changing. I leave out of account altogether the relation of this to the actual truth about the reign of Louis XI. But in fictional terms this uncertainty, this feeling of decline from an earlier high point of honour and courage provides a core of serious interest in a book marred, like the others, by sensationalism and haste. Scott does not forget that there are always people who have an interest in saying that there has been a decline. Thus Lady Hameline speaks of the Rhinegrave Godfrey who "won the hand of her Isabelle's grandmother by proving himself the best son of chivalry, at the great tournament of Strasbourg. Ten knights were slain in the lists. But those days are over, and no one now thinks of encountering peril for the sake of honour, or to relieve distressed beauty.

To this speech, which was made in the tone in which a modern beauty whose charms are rather on the wane, may be heard to condemn the rudeness of the present age, Quentin took upon him to reply, 'That there was no lack of that chivalry which the Lady Hameline seemed to consider as extinct . . .' "[2]

Despite some melodramatic extras, then, the central relationship in the book, between Louis XI and the Duke of Burgundy, is seriously conceived. The Duke knows that he is the stronger party and in a position to dictate terms. But

[1] *ibid* chap 10. [2] *Quentin Durward* chap 17.

he cannot escape altogether from the idea that the King of France is his superior by right, irrespective of power. Thus he orders the King to appear before him in tones which may not be disobeyed, but grants him a throne higher than his own when the meeting takes place. All this is well done; but it is just at points like this where the true Scott, the profound intelligence that triumphed in *Waverley*, seems to be once again at work, that we are disappointed. The point made is too general. The deep insight required into the mind of the Duke, and into the nature of the changing society, is lacking. We are left on the one hand with a sketch of great possibilities, largely unused, on the other, with an exciting tale of little lasting significance. This would be a fair summary of several other novels, too. It would cover the antagonism between Norman and Saxon in *Ivanhoe*, and the potentially interesting political situation between Douglas and March in *The Fair Maid of Perth*, as well as the more perfunctorily treated struggle of the courtiers in *Kenilworth*.

But there are times when the anti-romantic tendency, already noted in the treatment of the hero of *Quentin Durward*, has consequences that mark Scott off very sharply from other mediaevalists. Wilkin, the Flemish weaver in *The Betrothed*, and his daughter Rose provide a striking case. In the passage that follows Rose is trying to dissuade her mistress from promising to marry the man who has led the defence of her castle against attack.

" 'He is too great to be loved himself—too haughty to love you as you deserve. If you wed him, you wed gilded misery, and, it may be, dishonour as well as discontent.'

'Remember, damsel,' answered Eveline Berenger, 'his services towards us.'

'His services?' answered Rose. 'He ventured his life for us, indeed, but so did every soldier in his host. And am I bound to wed any ruffling blade among them, because he fought when the trumpet sounded? I wonder what is the meaning of their *devoir*, as they call it, when it shames them not to claim the highest reward a woman can bestow, merely for discharging the duty of a gentleman, by a distressed creature. A gentleman, said I?—The coarsest boor in Flanders would hardly expect thanks for doing the duty of a man by women in such a case.' "[1]

The speech of the characters here, as so often in Scott's mediaeval works, is a slack Wardour Street, full of dead clichés. This was almost inevitable, since he did not know how mediaeval people really spoke, and since no doubt his readers would have felt cheated if they had spoken in contemporary style. But if we overlook the unreality of the idiom, and look to the substance of what is being said, we are faced with something both intelligent and original. It is nothing less than a serious critique of the insincerities and ambiguities of the knightly code. It grasps firmly the selfish core within humble professions of service, the class arrogance that claims for a gentleman a power to love differently from others, the brute male strength which is unmentioned but really present in the chivalrous devotion.

A similar point is made by Rose's father in his argument with De Lacy, the Constable, who is instructing him to ensure that no unauthorized person is allowed to communicate with Lady Eveline.

" 'By keeping the doors shut, I tell thee,' answered the Constable, still in the same tone of forced jocularity; 'a wooden bar will be thy warrant.'

'Ay, but,' answered Flammock, 'if the Flemish weaver say *shut*, when the Norman young lady says *open*, think which has best chance of being obeyed. At a word, my lord, for the matter of guardianship, and such like, I wash my hands of it—I would not undertake to be guardian to the chaste

---

[1] *The Betrothed* chap 12.

Susannah, though she lived in an enchanted castle which no living thing could approach.'

'Thou holdest the language and thoughts,' said De Lacy, 'of a vulgar debauchee, who laughs at female constancy, because he has lived only with the most worthless of the sex. Yet thou shouldst know the contrary, having, as I know, a most virtuous daughter——'

'Whose mother was not less so' said Wilkin, breaking in . . ."[1]

Wilkin shows an equal dignity, realism and impatience with knightly pretensions in military matters during the seige.

Scott was speaking here, as he had done with fuller knowledge and more subtle treatment in *Rob Roy*, of the dignity of the merchant class. His natural fairness and shrewdness made him see something which most authors who were his contemporaries, more dominated by fashion than he, or, like Byron, more directed by personal class feeling, refused to see. For all the highly-coloured surface of the mediaeval novels and their stilted speech, this is really a very far cry from damozels and knights-at-arms palely loitering.

There are times, too, when the calm, unillusioned view of the author himself adds its weight to the words of the Flemings. Here is the scene that follows a battle:

"That the spoil thus acquired might not long encumber the soldier, or blunt his ardour for farther enterprise, the usual means of dissipating military spoils were already at hand. Courtezans, mimes, jugglers, minstrels and tale-tellers of every description, had accompanied the night-march; and secure in the military reputation of the celebrated De Lacy, had rested fearlessly at some little distance until the battle was fought and won. These now approached, in many a joyous group, to congratulate the victors. Close to the parties

---

[1] *ibid* chap 21.

which they formed for the dance, the song, or the tale, upon
the yet bloody field, the countrymen, summoned in for
the purpose, were opening large trenches for depositing the
dead—leeches were seen tending the wounded—priests and
monks confessing those in extremity—soldiers transporting
from the field the bodies of the more honoured among the
slain—peasants mourning over their trampled crops and
plundered habitations—and widows and orphans searching
for the bodies of husbands and parents . . ."[1]

This indeed is life, not escape. But again, it is a *general*
statement. It is touching and true, but it is not illuminating
about one time and place rather than another. It is really a
sign of the failure of these books as novels that such broad,
meditative passages, which could occur in an essay as appropriately as in a novel, are often the most memorable.
Their presence may even increase our irritation at finding a
man capable of this large, clear view of life as it is, engaged
in puerilities. For puerility is hardly an unfair word for the
'Benedicite' language of his monks, or the fantastic resolu-
tions required by some of the plots.

Here again we are confronted with the basic cause of
failure. To write a historical novel of any importance an
author needs to know a great deal about his period. He
needs much more information than he will ever actually use.
He needs in G. M. Young's words "to read until he can hear
people talking". Scott possessed this sort of knowledge about
as far back as the reign of Charles II, in which one of his
greatest books, *Old Mortality*, and one of his partial successes,
Peveril of the Peak, are laid. Beyond that he never had it, and
his earlier periods tend to merge into one. The twelfth century
of *Ivanhoe* is nearer to the sixteenth in *Kenilworth* than the
latter is to the finely realized late seventeenth century Scotland of *Old Mortality*.

[1] *ibid* chap 10.

Usually, what takes the place of the absent historical insight is an uneasy kind of ventriloquism or historical substitution. Either the words of the character, monk or king or baron, are recognizably the words of Walter Scott, or else they are not his own words but the words of a much later form of civilization, thinly disguised. A few examples from *Ivanhoe* should make this clear. Thus Rebecca, the noble Jewess, bids farewell to Rowena: " 'Lady,' she said, 'the countenance you have deigned to show me will long dwell in my remembrance. There reigns in it gentleness and goodness; and if a tinge of the world's pride or vanities may mix with an expression so lovely, how should we chide that which is of earth for bearing some colour of its original? Long, long will I remember your features, and bless God that I leave my noble deliverer united with——'

She stopped short—her eyes filled with tears."[1] However, it might be said that the rivalry of women, whether 'noble' or not, was hardly within Scott's range at any time. The following is a clearer case of the author almost forgetting who is supposed to be speaking:

" 'Rebecca,' said the Templar, 'dost thou hear me?'

'I have no portion in thee, cruel, hard-hearted man,' said the unfortunate maiden.

'Ay, but dost thou understand my words?' said the Templar; 'for the sound of my own voice is frightful in mine own ears. I scarce know on what ground we stand, or for what purpose they have brought us hither. This listed space —that chair—these faggots—I know their purpose, and yet it appears to me like something unreal—the fearful picture of a vision, which appals my sense with hideous fantasies, but convinces not my reason.'

'My mind and senses keep touch and time,' answered Rebecca, 'and tell me alike that these faggots are destined

---

[1] *Ivanhoe* chap 44.

to consume my earthly body, and open a painful but a brief passage to a better world.'

'Dreams, Rebecca—dreams,' answered the Templar— 'idle visions, rejected by the wisdom of your own wiser Sadducees. Hear me, Rebecca,' he said, proceeding with animation; 'a better chance hast thou for life and liberty than yonder knaves and dotard dream of. Mount thee behind me on my steed—on Zamor, the gallant horse that never failed his rider.' "[1]

It is an interesting point in the history of taste that generations of boys appear to have read stuff like this with excitement and even ecstasy. But it is not only unreal; it is an amalgam of different kinds of unreality with transitions of the most abrupt kind. What is one to say of a twelfth century brute who talks like a self-conscious sea-captain in a boys' story, but turns aside for a moment to refer to an obscure Hebrew heresy of the first century A.D.? Speeches like this show Scott almost appearing to forget that he is a novelist and allotting the contents of his well-stocked mind with impartial abandon to male and female, to lustful and chaste, villain and heroine.

Many other such passages could be produced. It would be wrong to dwell on them; any author is entitled to demand that we pay more attention to his best than his worst. But to fail to mention them at all would be to miss two important points. One is that Scott like several other great English writers was something of a somnambulist. A hasty writer, a busy man of the world, a man both modest about his own intellectual powers, and delighted by his great popular success, he seldom knew whether he was writing well or ill. It is likely that he overrated a passage like that just quoted as much as he underrated his finest achievements. In this insensitivity to his own literary merits and defects he resembles

[1] *ibid* chap 43.

Byron in his own time and a number of Victorian writers, notably Dickens. It might be an interesting question for scholarship—one for which I have neither the space nor the learning—whether or not this is, in the main, a new and characteristic development of the nineteenth century, or whether it is perennial and springs from the familiar difficulty of 'the subject as object'. Whatever the right answer to this question, it is clear that Scott is a very extreme case of this ignorance of his own achievement and of his own failure.

The other important point has been briefly mentioned already. A passage like the above exchange between Rebecca and the Templar, coming as it does at the climax of one of Scott's most popular works, could well lead the most sensitive critic astray. Life is short, and books (especially in the nineteenth century) are many. There must be many, capable of enjoying what is best in Scott, who have read passages like this and absolved themselves from further enquiry. It is certainly strange, but I hope that it is by now intelligible, that the same man should have written this and (say) the account of the battle of Drumclog in *Old Mortality*.

The same carelessness can be seen in the use of sources in many of these late books. *Count Robert of Paris*, dealing with Byzantine history of which Scott had no special knowledge, relies heavily on Gibbon. In the first chapter we are told that the official adoption of Christianity in the fourth century was 'unspeakably to the advantage' of Byzantium, because, "The world was now Christian, and, with the Pagan code, had got rid of its load of disgraceful superstition. Nor is there the least doubt, that the better faith produced its natural and desirable fruits in society, in gradually ameliorating the hearts and taming the passions of the people." In fact, on the question which is central to Gibbon's whole interpretation he says exactly the opposite of what Gibbon says. But, within a page or two, he is saying: "Constantinople, therefore, when in 324 it first arose in imperial majesty out of the humble Byzantium, showed, even in its birth, and amid its adventitious splendour . . . some intimations of that speedy decay to which the whole civilized world, then limited within the Roman empire, was internally and imperceptibly tending." In fact, Scott agrees exactly with Gibbon's general view.

It seems extraordinary that a man so intelligent should have so little intellectual curiosity here. If Gibbon is exactly right, but the main reason he gives is exactly wrong, a most interesting set of questions arises. Scott does not ask himself any of them, but labours steadily on with the task of covering blank paper with ink.

In saying 'it seems extraordinary', I meant so long as we are looking only at the text of *Count Robert*. But if we turn to Scott's journal for May 8, 1831, the day after the publishers warned him the public would not like *Count Robert*, it will seem much more natural. He writes: "I have suffered terribly, that is the truth, rather in body than in mind, and I often wish I could lie down and sleep without waking. But I will fight it out if I can. It would argue too great an attachment of consequence to my literary labours to sink under . . . After all, this but fear and faintness of heart, though of another kind from that which trembleth at a loaded pistol. My bodily strength is terribly gone; perhaps my mental too?"

Reading that, and knowing that the writer was not inclined by nature to dramatize himself, we shall hardly judge with severity the lack of real attention to Gibbon's argument.

It is not surprising after all this, to find that there are times when the very intention of writing historically seems to falter. The author's convenience is allowed to play havoc with chronology. Scott's note 31 to *Quentin Durward* is typical of a large number of cases of a curious deliberate and determined neglect of the nature of the task he had set himself. He writes: "In assigning the present date to the murder of the Bishop of Liege, Louis de Bourbon, history has been violated. It is true that the bishop was made prisoner by the insurgents of that city. It is also true that the report of the insurrection came to Charles with a rumour that the bishop was slain, which excited his indignation against Louis, who was then in his power. But these things happened in 1467, and the bishop's murder did not take place till 1482 . . . The murder of the bishop has been fifteen years antedated in the text, for reasons which the reader of romances will easily appreciate." That last sentence is very characteristic. One does not know whether to be irritated by the easy manner of the popular idol, who knows that his wares are quite good enough to sell, or to admire that genuine modesty, that casual attitude to his own genius that was one of the most marked traits in his nature, and in such striking contrast to the self-importance of his great contemporaries.

In either case, we must recognize that we are dealing here not just with a casual remark in a note, but with a settled attitude to the writing of mediaeval fiction. He states it most clearly in his essay on the novels of Clara Reeve, whose *Old English Baron* is full of obvious anachronisms. He defends her by saying: "He that would please the modern world, yet present the exact impression of the middle ages, will repeatedly find that he will be obliged, in despite of his utmost exertions, to sacrifice the last to the first object, and eternally expose himself to the just censure of the rigid antiquary, because he must, to interest the readers of the present time, invest his characters with language and sentiments unknown to the period assigned to his story; and thus his utmost efforts only attain a sort of composition between the true and the fictitious,—just as the dress of Lear, as performed on the stage, is neither that of a modern sovereign, nor the cerulean painting and bear-hide with which the Britons, at the time when that monarch is supposed to have lived, tattooed their persons, and sheltered themselves from cold. All this inconsistency is avoided by adopting the style of our grandfathers and great-grandfathers, sufficiently antiquated to accord with the antiquated character of the narrative, yet copious enough to express all that is necessary to its interest, and to supply that deficiency of colouring which the more ancient times do not afford."[1]

Many comments could be made. We might say that such a plan was perhaps good enough for Clara Reeve, but not for the vastly greater creative energies of Walter Scott. We might complain that the word 'antiquaries' begs the question, for the crucial word 'sentiments' tacitly admits that it is not just superficial details but the whole stuff of history that is being violated. For 'sentiments' is for Scott a much more impressive word than it is for us. It involves the whole way men thought and felt about the world—everything, in fact, which makes history, and hence historical fiction, interesting. We might note that the mention of *King Lear* is something of a red herring, because the theatre can in any case hardly attempt the fully historical treatment which Scott achieved in his seventeenth- and eighteenth-century settings, and that Shakespeare in *King Lear* did not erect any of that laborious pseudo-historical structure which exists in all Scott's mediaeval novels, and which he is here almost admitting to be a waste of time.

But perhaps the simplest and best thing to say is that Scott is here admitting, in effect, that his mediaeval novels were not meant very seriously. For what, after all, can be the serious point of a mediaeval novel without distinctive mediaeval features, but full of the detailed pretence of being mediaeval? Scott is really admitting that in a large part of his writing life he was playing a game with the public. If we accept this, and we do because it answers exactly to our experience of reading many of the books, then his status as a

[1] *Prose Works* III p333-4.

real historical novelist is actually enhanced. For we are enabled to make a clearer division between the best and the worst in Scott. Scott was good precisely when his method was truly historical. It could only be that when he knew enough and felt enough about the period with which he dealt to recreate the past with imaginative insight. He could only do this for times within about a hundred years of his own boyhood. 1679, the imagined date of *Old Mortality*, is about the furthest reach of a process which relied largely on oral tradition. Most characteristically, the process works with shorter periods than this, as in *Waverley* and *Red-gauntlet*. It would be difficult to overestimate the importance of the experience of actually listening to the reminiscences of the old man who became the model for Baron Bradwardine. So, when considering Scott the man we must take his mediaeval interests into account; when considering the actual influence of Scott on generations of readers up till about 1914, we must take it into account. But when we think of his great and enduring contribution to our literature, we can forget it with relief.

PART TWO

The Major Novels

1 *Waverley*

More than most historical subjects the Jacobite rebellion of 1745 would seem to dictate to any novelist attempting it the main structure of his story. Prince Charles' men won a victory, marched as far as Derby, then retreated, and suffered a defeat, which proved finally fatal to their cause. This simple outline of events is perfectly adapted to a strong and simple and immensely venerable literary treatment. It invites those two contrasted movements of rise and fall, growth and decay which are equally serviceable for a study of a Greek tyrant, or for Macbeth, or for a business-man of Balzac. This, one would think, is a tradition that cannot be outmoded because, while capable of infinite variety, it corresponds all the time to experiences fundamental to life as we know it, to the progression of the seasons, and the cycle of infancy, manhood, old-age and death. For all his learning and his subtlety, there is no doubt that Scott responded with simple sincerity to what one might call the platitudinous sublime; it is a mode of thought and feeling often to be found in the more intense prophetic passages of characters like Meg Merrilies and Edie Ochiltree.

So the most interesting general problem about the structure of *Waverley* is, 'Why did not Scott adopt a formal pattern, so simple and flexible, so much in keeping with the historical facts, and (so far as one has the right to judge this) in harmony with the general constitution of his mind?'

We experience the story through Waverley himself, and

107

Waverley's first experience of the Jacobite ideal is weak, diffused, etiolated. His uncle, in whose library he first reads the old romances, is not at all the sort of Jacobite we find later in the book. He has neither the steadfast antiquarian honour of Bradwardine, nor (still less) the energy and ambition of Fergus Mac-Ivor. The speech he makes in sending Waverley out into the world shows that he regards Jacobite loyalty as a sweet sentiment of former days, something that cannot be expected to appeal, even as a sentiment, to the young who cannot remember 1715 or to influence practical decisions for anyone, young or old. He is sending his nephew and heir to serve him whom Jacobites call the Elector of Hanover.

‘ "I have made such arrangements as will enable you to take the field as their descendant [the former military Waverleys], and as the probable heir of the house of Waverley; and, sir, in the field of battle you will remember what name you bear. And, Edward, my dear boy, remember also that you are the last of that race, and that the only hope of its revival depends upon you; therefore, as far as duty and honour will permit, avoid danger—I mean unnecessary danger—and keep no company with rakes, gamblers, and Whigs, of whom, it is to be feared, there are too many in the service into which you are going. Your colonel, as I am informed, is an excellent man—for a Presbyterian; but you will remember your duty to God, the Church of England, and the" (this breach ought to have been supplied, according to the rubrick, with the word *king*; but as, unfortunately that word conveyed a double and embarrassing sense, one meaning *de facto*, and the other *de jure*, the knight filled up the blank otherwise)—"the Church of England, and all constituted authorities."[1] Sir Everard is a dreamer about the past, but an extremely prudent one. He may say that he

[1] *Waverley* chap 6.

regrets the decline of feudal feeling since the days of the legendary Sir Hildebrand Waverley, but it is obvious that feudal feeling would be incompatible with the canny, practical advice he offers to his nephew. The first impression the reader must receive of the Jacobite cause is that it is dead; and that its faded memory provides a reserve area of feeling for lonely old men whose real practical rule of conduct is very different, and runs like this: "Don't bother about courage, honour and glory more than a soldier must to win respect and promotion." One would have thought all this more suited to the sunset world of *Redgauntlet*, where the Jacobites are too weak to raise an army and are treated by the Hanoverian authorities with benevolent contempt. For, in *Waverley*, once we are introduced to Fergus Mac-Ivor and the Prince, we are in the presence of an active and flourishing cause, led by young men, possessing a reasonable share of practical ability and realism. But Scott had his reasons.

When Waverley reaches Tully-Veolan, the home of Baron Bradwardine, and the first Jacobite stronghold he visits, the image of social decay is immediately added to his uncle's decaying will and loyalty.

"The houses seemed miserable in the extreme, especially to an eye accustomed to the smiling neatness of English cottages. They stood without any respect for regularity, on each side of a straggling kind of unpaved street, where children, almost in a primitive state of nakedness, lay sprawling, as if to be crushed by the hoofs of the first passing horse . . . The whole scene was depressing; for it argued, at the first glance, at least a stagnation of industry, and perhaps of intellect. Even curiosity, the busiest passion of the idle, seemed of a listless cast in the village of Tully-Veolan: the curs alone showed any part of its activity."[1]

Scott has a surprise in store for us here. This, we are meant

[1] Chap 8.

to think, is the hopeless soil of the Highlands, in which the moribund cause favoured by Waverley's uncle is perishing for ever. This natural assumption will prove to be erroneous in several ways. First, this is not the Highlands at all, but the edge of the Lowlands exposed to the depredations of Highland cattle-raiders. Then this apparent home of ignorance proves to be a place of learning. Bradwardine is no barbarian, but a pedantic scholar, caring not only for the records and quarterings of his own lineage, but for Livy and Virgil, in fact for the fundamental European culture, which underlies and outlasts all differences between English and Scot, Highland and Lowland, Jacobite and Hanoverian. (This point Scott has in reserve, for use much later.)

In part, of course, this is a familiar point of technique in the adventure story. We are first persuaded that something is the extreme of strangeness, and then we are shown something else which makes the first wonder seem, by comparison, ordinary. We are to move through layers of strangeness towards the barbarous Highland hiding-places. But there is more to it than that. It prepares the way for the second major eccentricity in the book's structure. What we are expecting is a contrast between Highland and English culture, and between Jacobite and Hanoverian politics. We get this only intermittently and indirectly. The characters who might show the Hanoverian side, the loyal English, the Scots Whigs and the Cameronians are all minor figures. Waverley's father barely appears. Gilfillan, the Cameronian, has a vivid scene, but soon disappears from the story for good. Colonel Gardiner is killed almost before we have got to know him. We know from *Old Mortality* and *Rob Roy* that Scott was deeply interested in the Covenanters, and Lowland Whigs; it is clear that we have here not a blurred impression due to lack of understanding or to haste but a calculated omission.

These obvious contrasts are left out because they would overshadow the subtler contrast that Scott is intent on giving us, that between Bradwardine and Fergus Mac-Ivor. For Bradwardine the point of honour is everything. He has the legal right, and, of course, a strong desire to leave his estate to his daughter, instead of to an almost unknown male relative. "But the Baron would not listen to such a proposal for an instant. On the contrary, he used to have a perverse pleasure in boasting that the barony of Bradwardine was a male fief, the first charter having been given at that early period when women were not deemed capable to hold a feudal grant . . . He would triumphantly ask, how it would become a female, and that female a Bradwardine, to be seen employed *in servitio exuendi, seu detrahendi caligas regis post battaliam?* that is, in pulling off the king's boots after an engagement, which was the feudal service by which he held the barony of Bradwardine. 'No,' he said, 'beyond hesitation, *procul dubio,* many females as worthy as Rose, have been excluded in order to make way for my own succession . . .'"[1] The pride of lineage, so often in Scott presented as a tiresome piece of nonsense, (in the case of Lady Margaret Bellenden, for instance) here has an element of Quixotic generosity. Scott's admiration for this does not, however, in the least cloud his sense of realities. So he shows us how meanly this favoured relative will repay the Baron's chivalrous solicitude for his interests when the rebellion has failed, and the estates are forfeit. And even the most unreasonable and degraded article in the code of aristocratic honour, the settling of drunken quarrels by duelling, is endued with a touch of generosity by the Baron. For he saves his guest, Waverley, from danger by taking his quarrel with Balmawhapple upon himself, on the plea that the host is personally responsible for the protection of his guest.

Our first introduction to Fergus Mac-Ivor is very different. Some of the Baron's cows have been stolen, and, says his

[1] Chap 14.

daughter, "We used to be quite free from them while we paid black-mail to Fergus Mac-Ivor Vich Ian Vohr; but my father thought it unworthy of his rank and birth to pay it any longer . . ."[1] The theory of the honour of cattle-thieving, practised by Donald Bean Lean, and connived at, or encouraged by Mac-Ivor, when the blackmail has not been paid, is explained to Waverley a little later by Fergus' faithful henchman and foster-brother, Evan Dhu Maccombich: "Common thief!—No such thing: Donald Bean Lean never lifted less than a drove in his life."

"Do you call him an uncommon thief, then?"

"No—he that steals a cow from a poor widow, or a stirk from a cottar, is a thief; he that lifts a drove from a Sassenach laird, is a gentleman drover."[2] The justification of this, in Maccombich's mind, lies in the danger. It is an offence that carries the death penalty, and therefore has the same honourable character as war or duelling.

We have to reflect here upon the multiple incongruity of the standards by which men live. The impression we are rapidly forming of a gang of brave but brutal cattle thieves is first checked when Waverley asks Maccombich, "Do others beside your master shelter him?" "My master?—*My* master is in Heaven," answered Evan, haughtily; and then immediately assuming his usual civility of manner, "but you mean my Chief;—no . . ."

This reply does not only show a religious sense, but also a high, civilized consideration for the feelings of a guest. This point too Scott has in reserve. When the Jacobite cause is lost, and Fergus Mac-Ivor is on trial for his life, Evan will show in their full force this strange and moving combination of barbaric loyalty and civilized dignity:

" 'If your excellent honour, and the honourable court, would let Vich Ian Vohr go free just this once, and let him

1 Chap 15.　　2 Chap 18.

gae back to France, and no to trouble King George's government again, thar ony six o' the very best of his clan will be
willing to be justified in his stead; and if you'll just let me gae
down to Glennaquoich, I'll fetch them up to ye mysell, to
head or hang, and you may begin wi' me the very first man.'

Notwithstanding the solemnity of the occasion, a sort of
laugh was heard in the court at the extraordinary nature of
the proposal. The Judge checked this indecency, and Evan,
looking sternly round, when the murmur abated, 'If the
Saxon gentlemen are laughing', he said, 'because a poor
man, such as me, thinks my life, or the life of six of my degree
is worth that of Vich Ian Vohr, it's like enough they may be
very right; but if they laugh because they think I would not
keep my word, and come back to redeem him, I can tell
them they ken neither the heart of a Hielandman, nor the
honour of a gentleman.'

There was no further inclination to laugh among the
audience and a dead silence ensued."[1] How typical of Scott
it is that he should present the most purely heroic scene in
the book through the lens of the uncomprehending, self-
satisfied English observers with their uneasy laughter, and
their sudden moment of unwilling respect. That great climax
is far in the future, as Waverley talks to Evan for the first
time. It is quoted here to show how effectively (and how unobtrusively) some of Scott's great scenes are prepared.

But for the moment, Evan's words to Waverley reveal to
him that the feudal loyalty that his uncle had so feebly re-
gretted is here a reality:

"Well, but when you were in King George's pay, Evan,
you were surely King George's soldiers?"

"Troth, and you must ask Vich Ian Vohr about that; for
we are for his king, and care not much which o' them it
is."[2]

[1] Chap 68.   [2] Chap 18.

But the real surprise comes when we meet Vich Ian Vohr (Mac-Ivor) himself. He is indeed, as we had expected, hard, brave and ruthless. But he is also a calculating politician with a cosmopolitan background. His mother had been French, and the paternal estate had been repurchased after his father's exile in 1715, not continuously held. Like all men of affairs, who are neither perfectly honest, nor entirely un-principled, he makes his conception of honour, and of loyalty to the 'true king', serve his interest. Hoping for an earldom, he "easily reconciled his conscience to going certain lengths in the service of his party, from which honour and pride would have deterred him, had his sole object been the direct advancement of his own personal interest." He sees clearly that the cattle-thieving and general lawlessness are to his interest, because "government, which has removed other means of defence, must connive at our protecting ourselves." He knows that if the country were once in a state of peace, his reward would be "a summons to deliver up to General Blakeney, at Stirling, the few broadswords they have left us."[1]

The more displeasing side of Fergus' calculations is seen in his attitude to women. Of his beautiful sister's presence in Edinburgh with the Prince's 'court' he says: "I thought it better she should come here, as since our success a good many ladies of rank attend our military court; and I assure you, that there is a sort of consequence annexed to the near relative of such a person as Flora Mac-Ivor, and where there is such a justling of claims and requests, a man must use every fair means to enhance his importance."[2] This kind of in-sensibility is attributed by Scott mainly to his upbringing in the French court. In one sense, Fergus is not too barbarous but too civilized. The Jacobite cause is a strange coalition of tribal simplicities and worldly calculations, together with the scholarly, conservative loyalty represented by Brad-

[1] Chap 19.   [2] Chap 41.

wardine. The principle of hereditary tribal loyalty, which Mac-Ivor, just before his death at Carlisle, recalls in the words 'Vich Ian Vohr—the only *Open Sesame* to their feelings and sympathies', is leading paradoxically to a complete separation of culture and outlook between the Chief and his followers. And what is true on the small scale is true also on the great, as we see when the Pretender himself, the focus of all the traditional loyalties says: "Que mon métier de prince errant est ennuyant, par fois. Mais courage! c'est le grand jeu, après tout."[1] Scott knew what he was doing when he put those words and no others into the French language.

Scott is presenting the old blind loyalty as near the end of its term, partly because the response of the leader can no longer have the old simplicity. "Had Fergus Mac-Ivor lived Sixty Years sooner than he did, he would, in all probability, have wanted the polished manner and knowledge of the world which he now possessed, and had he lived Sixty Years later, his ambition and love of rule would have lacked the fuel which his situation now afforded."[2]

We are nearer now, I think, to understanding how sound was Scott's surprising choice of structure for his story. The absence of the hero from the later part of the military campaign, the rather cursory treatment of Culloden and miseries that followed it is right for what Scott was attempting. He wished to show us the inherent collapse of the old Highland values, and not to derive the false impression that a mere military defeat was the cause. Hence the strange choice of the dreamy, ineffective Sir Edward Waverley to introduce the Jacobite cause to us. The movement of the book, instead of using the obvious pattern of rise and fall, which we have already seen that Scott rejected, is really constructed in a circle. It moves from Waverley dreaming over romantic books in his uncle's library, from a family attachment to the

[1] Chap 58.   [2] Chap 19.

Jacobite cause which is merely sentimental, through the stirring days of the rebellion itself, when the Jacobite cause seems for a time to become a reality, and the round and back to the much more poignant and deeply-felt nostalgia of the defeated Jacobite, who has sacrified so much for the cause: "It grieves me sometimes to look upon these blackened walls of the house of my ancestors; but doubtless officers cannot always keep the soldier's hand from depredation and spuilzie . . . To be sure we may say with Virgilius Maro, *Fuimus Troes*—and there's the end of an old sang. But houses and families and men have a' stood lang eneugh when they have stood till they fall with honour; and now I hae gotten a house that is not unlike a *domus ultima*. We poor Jacobites are now like the conies in Holy Scripture (which the great traveller Pococke called Jerboa,) a feeble people, that make our abode in the rocks."[1]

This is the moment when the Baron's Latin studies are suddenly made to tell, in a way we could not have guessed when we were first introduced to them. Instead of appearing merely bookish, he now has a right to his quotation. Like the Trojans in the midst of the burning of their city[2] he has devoted all his strength to try to save a civilization which is now ending. Perhaps Scott, who, after all, was no Jacobite himself,[3] had it in mind here that as the Trojans would become Romans, so the Jacobites would become a true part of Britain. But if he did, he was no doubt right not to make the point explicit, because at the moment of the failure of all one's hopes, all distant, slow consolations must seem impossible or irrelevant.

[1] Chap 65. The Baron is comparing his hiding-place, a burrow in which there is scarcely room to move, both to a rabbit-hole and to his own grave.
[2] Virgil, *Aeneid* II, 325.
[3] That is, not as a man and a citizen, but only as a dreamer and antiquarian. See above, chap 1.

The contrast between Mac-Ivor and Bradwardine, then, is not merely one between a high and a low conception of honour, but between two different kinds of alienation from society. The Frenchified Fergus regards the fervent loyalty of the clan towards himself as a private political advantage, and has quite a callous attitude to the personal interests of his devoted followers:

"That gallows-bird's skull,' said Fergus, "must be harder than marble: the lock of the pistol was actually broken."

"How could you strike so young a lad so hard?" said Waverley, with some interest.

"Why, if I did not strike hard sometimes, the rascals would forget themselves."[1]

At the same time he has enough Highland atavism to accept without question that the appearance of the family apparition must herald his capture or death. There is a subtle difference between the manner of his death, and that of his foster-brother Evan Maccombich at Carlisle. When Fergus replies to the official cry of 'God save King George' with 'God save King James', he is sticking to his colours in defeat as any brave soldier will do. He has staked all and lost. But Evan MacCombich's offer of his own and five other lives to save Mac-Ivor's is the true, desperate blind loyalty and devotion, which Fergus could never feel. When new adherents had joined the Jacobite cause during their march south, Fergus had "always considered them in the light of new claimants upon the favours of the future monarch, who, he concluded, must therefore subtract for their gratification so much of the bounty which ought to be shared among his Highland followers."[2]

Every reader of *Waverley* has enjoyed the rich absurdity of the scene where the Baron performs his traditional feudal service to the Prince by taking off his boots. But the comedy

[1] Chap 59.   [2] Chap 57.

is superficial, the tragedy essential. There is a close and significant contrast between chapter 48, in which Bradwardine parades his learned doubts about the boots, and chapter 53, in which Fergus describes how he was disappointed in his suit to the Prince. Once again the author, in his friendly, unassuming way, is laying something of a trap for us. As the Baron pours out his interminable torrent of learning about the meaning of the Latin *caligae*, and the nature of the feudal tenures, "Fergus turned his falcon eye upon Edward, with an almost imperceptible rise of his eyebrow, to which his shoulders corresponded in the same degree of elevation." The unwary reader is with Fergus here, and may be expressing his disdain with less finesse. When the Baron wonders whether it is legitimate to substitute the boots of the Prince for those of the King, his absent father, Fergus says, that the Prince is the Regent (a doubtful point) and, "Were I to pull off either of their boots, I would render that service to the young Chevalier ten times more willingly than to his father."

"Ay", replies the Baron, "but I talk not of personal predilections . . ." This reply has great weight in the circumstances. What is the Jacobite cause supposed to be about? It is about unconditional, irrevocable loyalty. Anyone can see that it is much the most convenient and sensible thing to accept a government in power, to avoid bloodshed, to treat law and order as more important than historical precedent. The Jacobite cause only makes sense if it is a categorical imperative; if the forms of order and civilization laid down in the past are in principle unchangeable by one generation. If all that is true, then the old feudal services are a part of the fabric. True, this particular point is a small one; the Baron may fairly be convicted, on Jacobite principles, of lacking a sense of proportion. But Fergus' error is greater, it is a fundamental inconsistency of principle, and this we see more clearly in chapter 53. Fergus, after an interview with

118

the Prince, is angrily inclined to curse his adherence to the cause. Very neatly, Scott has enforced the contrast with chapter 48 by making the service of the *caligae* relevant to Fergus' complaint.

" 'Would you believe it, I made this very morning two suits to the Prince, and he has rejected them both; what do you think of it?'

'What can I think,' answered Waverley, 'till I know what your requests were?'

'Why, what signifies what they were, man? I tell you it was I that made them; I, to whom he owes more than to any three who have joined the standard; for I negotiated the whole business, and brought in all the Perthshire men when not one would have stirred. I am not likely, I think, to ask anything very unreasonable, and if I did, they might have stretched a point.—Well, but you shall know all, now that I can draw my breath again with some freedom.—You remember my earl's patent; it is dated some years back, for services then rendered; and certainly my merit has not been diminished, to say the least, by my subsequent behaviour. Now, sir, I value this bauble of a coronet as little as you can, or any philosopher on earth; for I hold that the chief of such a clan as the Sliochd nan Ivor is superior in rank to any earl in Scotland. But I had a particular reason for assuming this cursed title at this time. You must know that I learned accidentally that the Prince has been pressing that old foolish Baron of Bradwardine to disinherit his male heir, or nineteenth or twentieth cousin, who has taken a command in the Elector of Hanover's militia, and to settle his estate upon your pretty little friend Rose; and this as being the command of his king and overlord, who may alter the destination of a fief at pleasure, the old gentleman seems well reconciled to.'

"And what becomes of the homage?"

"Curse the homage!—I believe Rose is to pull off the

queen's slipper on her coronation-day, or some such trash. Well, sir, as Rose Bradwardine would always have made a suitable match for me, but for this idiotical predilection of her father for the heir-male, it occurred to me there now remained no obstacle, unless that the Baron might expect his daughter's husband to take the name Bradwardine, (which you know would be impossible in my case,) and that this might be evaded by my assuming the title to which I had so good a right, and which, of course, would supersede that difficulty."[1]

As if to underline his view that all sentiment is nonsense, Fergus goes on to say that his affection for Rose is very moderate. It is obvious that Fergus in defeat has a much narrower and more conventional range of pathos than that which Bradwardine expresses in the 'Fuimus Troes' speech. But there is one reason why this pathos is greater than that of any brave man who has staked his life and lost. He is a calculating Jacobite, because that is his temperament; an inconsistent one because he has never thought about the implications of the Jacobite theory of loyalty. But he might never have been one at all but for the influence of his sister. Without her, the spectrum of Jacobite mentalities would be incomplete. What to her brother is politics, and to Bradwardine is the justice of ancient right, is to her pure romance. It is obvious that she is much nearer in feeling to the nostalgic memory of the Jacobite cause which so many of Scott's first readers must have felt. We see her first, through Waverley's eyes, very much as many of Scott's readers must have delighted to see her, the high-born Highland maiden, wild and pure, against a background of waterfalls and misty mountains. Once again there is a trap here. It is not a satirical trap. Scott is far too generous a man, and far too sensitive to the poignancy of lost causes to make fun of this

[1] Chap 53.

conception. And it may be that some unwary readers derived this impression of Flora, *simpliciter*, unmodified by what follows. But the book as a whole gives a much more complex analysis. From our earlier knowledge of Flora we expect that she will mourn her brother only as a Roman matron would mourn her son honourably killed in battle, that she will feel that he is happier than herself in having the male privilege of perishing for and with the cause. Instead, when Waverley goes to see her after her brother's condemnation she says:

"There is a busy devil at my heart, that whispers—but it were madness to listen to it—that the strength of mind on which Flora prided herself has murdered her brother!"

"Good God! how can you give utterance to a thought so shocking?"

"Ay, is it not so? but yet it haunts me like a phantom; I know it is unsubstantial and vain; but it *will* be present; will intrude its horrors on my mind; will whisper that my brother, as volatile as ardent, would have divided his energies amid a hundred objects. It was I who taught him to concentrate them, and to gage all on this dreadful and desperate cast. Oh, that I could recollect that I had once said to him, 'He that striketh by the sword, shall die by the sword;' that I had but once said, 'Remain at home; reserve yourself, your vassals, your life, for enterprises within the reach of man.' "[1]

Many strands of Scott's complex personality combine to make this passage what it is. Only a man who felt the romantic appeal of the Jacobite cause to the full could have drawn Flora with such sympathy. But only a man with great gifts of psychological penetration, and an unusually strong sense of the implacable consequences of things could have eschewed this obvious opportunity for a grand emotional

[1] Chap 68.

climax, and given us instead this disturbing, enigmatic chapter. The combination of effects is subtle, but, as so often with Scott, an important element is a shrewd, even tough realism. He is showing us that it is fatal to attach oneself to a risky, romantic cause, unless the attachment is absolute. A martyr whose commitment to the cause is not total, is merely, like Fergus, one who has backed a loser. Flora herself was capable of being that complete martyr; but the sacrifice was not demanded of her, but of one who could not give it, though he could die bravely without a tremor.

Scott's uncomfortably discerning realism goes even further than this, for her brother in his last hour foresees that Flora may in the course of time overcome these terrible self-reproaches, and imagine Fergus as the true martyr he knows he never was. "She will then think of Fergus as of the heroes of our race, upon whose deeds she loved to dwell."[1] The story does not reach so far, but we may guess that he is right.

But for the moment, at least, she has escaped all deceptions, and sees everything as it is. And she says, "I do not regret his attempt, because it was wrong! O no! on that point I am armed; but because it was impossible it could end otherwise than thus."[2] That last sentence is Scott's verdict also, and, as we have seen, serves to explain the scanty treatment of the machinery of the Hanoverian victory. Why could it not end otherwise? Because of the incompatibility between clan loyalty, and national unity. As Evan MacCombich explained to Waverley, the loyalty of the clan to Fergus Mac-Ivor is so strong that he could lead them into the army of any king he chose. It is the strength of Fergus as a tactical politician that he understands the nature of this loyalty. And so, as the fighting begins at Preston Pans he cries, "Forward, sons of Ivor, or the Camerons will draw first blood."[3] This

[1] Chap 69.   [2] Chap 68.   [3] Chap 46.

ferocious inward-looking loyalty is incompatible either with
social harmony, or with civilized standards of personal conduct. Hence the murderous attack on Waverley when he is
wrongly supposed to have trifled with Flora's affections. But
the key passage here is perhaps to be found just before the
battle of Preston Pans. Waverley, hearing the cry of a mor-
tally wounded man for water, recognizes a member of his
old regiment, son of a tenant of the Waverley-Honour estate.
At this moment Fergus returns with the news that the Prince
is preparing for battle within two hours.

" 'A moment,—a moment; this poor prisoner is dying;—
where shall I find a surgeon?'

'Why, where should you? We have none, you know, but
two or three French fellows, who, I believe, are little better
than *garçons apothécaires*.'

'But the man will bleed to death.'

'Poor fellow!' said Fergus, in a momentary fit of com-
passion; then instantly added, 'But it will be a thousand
men's fate before night; so come along.'

'I cannot; I tell you he is a son of a tenant of my uncle's.'

'O, if he's a follower of yours, he must be looked to . . .'

Waverley rather gained than lost in the opinion of the
Highlanders, by his anxiety about the wounded man. They
would not have understood the general philanthropy, which
rendered it almost impossible for Waverley to have passed
any person in such distress; but, as apprehending that the
sufferer was one of his *following*, they unanimously allowed
that Waverley's conduct was that of a kind and considerate
chieftain, who merited the attachment of his people."[1]

The phrase 'general philanthropy' has a much more frosty
sound to us than it had to Scott and his first readers; it should
not be allowed to disguise the fact that this scene, though
perfectly in accord with ordinary probabilities, is also an

[1] Chap 45.

acted parable. Behind it lie the words of the Gospel: "Inasmuch as ye have done it unto one of the least of these my brethren, ye have done it unto me."[1]

Scott's final considered judgment of the Jacobite cause is complex, and better seen in *Rob Roy* and *Redgauntlet* than here. But in *Waverley* there is a persistent inner debate, not only in the mind of the hero, but in the mind of the author. Taken as a whole, *Waverley* is not as hostile to the Jacobite cause as scenes like this might suggest.

We have seen that the men loyal to King George are shadowy figures through most of the book; and we have seen why. But when we have had time to grasp the full implications of the contrast between Fergus and Bradwardine, Scott at long last introduces a parallel movement. Just as Fergus and Bradwardine who fight on the same side are utterly different, so are Waverley and Talbot, on opposite sides, seen to be more and more alike. Each saves the other's life. In chapter 55 Waverley sees that the high romance of military sacrifice is not exclusively the prerogative of the Jacobites. Talbot has had to leave his wife pregnant and in danger of death, at the call of duty. Here Waverley takes a risk in granting a parole to his prisoner, before a proper authority can be secured. In chapter 62, the positions are reversed and Gardiner is planning a safe conduct to Scotland for Waverley. By now the ostensible contrast of character has come to seem superficial or even misleading. Waverley is the man, as Flora had contemptuously said, to 'admire the moon, and quote a stanza from Tasso', while Talbot, in Rose's words 'looks as if he thought no Scottish woman worth the trouble of handing her a cup of tea'. Flora's comment is perceptive and prophetic: "High and perilous enterprise is not Waverley's forte."[2] Soon we find that both Talbot and Waverley are taking the same cool, professional attitude:

[1] Matthew xxv 40.   [2] Chap 52.

"To confess the truth, though it may lower me in your opinion, I am heartily tired of the trade of war, and am, as Fletcher's Humorous Lieutenant says, 'even as weary of this fighting——' "

"Fighting! Pooh, what have you seen but a skirmish or two? Ah! if you saw war on the grand scale—sixty or a hundred thousand men in the field on each side!"

"I am not at all curious, Colonel. Enough says our homely English proverb, is as good as a feast. The plumed troops and the big war used to enchant me in poetry; but the night marches, vigils, couches under the wintry sky, and such accompaniments of the glorious trade, are not at all to my taste in practice; then for dry blows, I had *my* fill of fighting at Clifton, where I escaped by a hair's breadth half-a-dozen times; and you, I should think——" He stopped.

"Had enough of it at Preston? you mean to say," answered the Colonel, laughing: "but 'tis my vocation, Hal."[1]

The final act of their co-operation is seen when Talbot in an affectionate letter is able to give Waverley what he so strongly desires but could not have obtained himself, a Royal Pardon for Bradwardine.

What is the point of this carefully designed association of Waverley and Talbot? The answer would seem to lie deep in the complexity of Scott's personality, and in the corresponding complexity of those of his works which truly reflect it. No man responded more thoroughly than Scott to the romantic appeal of military glory. Without this strain he could not have written *Waverley*. But there was too in his personality, and in the book itself, a balancing sense of the futility and littleness of war, of the fundamental human character which is alike in friend and foe. And characteristically, he gives expression to this in several ways, both prosaically and imaginatively. The prose comes, a little unexpectedly,

[1] Chap 62.

from Flora Mac-Ivor, at the end of the conversation with Rose already quoted:

"For mere fighting, I believe all men (that is, who deserve the name) are pretty much alike; there is generally more courage required to run away. They have besides, when confronted with each other, a certain instinct for strife, as we see in other male animals, such as dogs, bulls and so forth."

This is the original Samuel Johnson in Scott. But the imaginative treatment of the same idea is subtler and finer. In chapter 47, just before the battle of Preston Pans, a mist covers the two armies, who become for a moment indistinguishable to the reader. Unrecognizable in all their wide differences of dress and culture, they become alike, just *men*, until "The sun, which was now risen above the horizon, dispelled the mist. The vapours rose like a curtain", and contrasts, military and social, are once more obvious as the battle begins.

Then Waverley sees: "A brief gleam of December's sun shone sadly on the broad heath, which, towards the spot where the great north-west road entered the enclosures of Lord Lonsdale's property, exhibited dead bodies of men and horses, and the usual companions of war, a number of carrion-crows, hawks and ravens." And a little later: "The followers of the camp had already stripped the dead of all they could carry away."[1]

It is soon obvious to every reader that Waverley is 'the man between', placed by education, sentiment and circumstance in a position where both Jacobite and Hanoverian loyalties can influence him. But he is also the man between in another sense. Both views of war successively or together tug at his feelings, the romance of courage and sacrifice, the misery and waste of mutual destruction.

[1] Chap 60.

The late introduction of Talbot into the story is right. It is only after Waverley has understood, by long experience of Mac-Ivor and Bradwardine, how different can be the motives for engaging in the same cause, that he can feel the full force of another idea, that at a deeper level the man on both sides are just the same. Similarly, it is only after Scott has shown that the issues involved in the result of the war were truly momentous, and some of its passions heroic, that he can, without depriving his subject of its true dignity, show that in another sense, war is just one among the things that suffering humanity endures.

This steady double focus is perhaps Scott's most important contribution to the novel of heroic action. Its successful use requires qualities of mind that are exceedingly rare. Without it, the historical novel is doomed either to the pedantry of the fictionalized thesis, or the triviality of the costume adventure story. It seems to me that we have to go on nearly a hundred years to Conrad's *Nostromo*, before we find the double focus used with a mastery and largeness of effect equal to this.

All Scott's best books have something of this double focus. But *Waverley* differs from the others in its final reluctance to take sides. It is open to us to find the book's master image in the acted parable of the dying soldier, whom Waverley tends and Mac-Ivor would have neglected if he had been an outsider. In that case we shall see the principle of clan loyalty as finally condemned. Or it is open to us to take the heroic view and find the master image in Bradwardine's lament and MacCombich's offer of his life at Carlisle. Scott has presented each image as powerfully as if it was the only one. In *Waverley*, then, the first and longest-pondered of his novels, the conflicting impulses of Scott's mind are held in equilibrium. In his later treatment of the Jacobite theme he was to specialize. *Rob Roy* concentrates on what was gained for the country in the Jacobite defeat; *Redgauntlet* is concerned with the question of loyalty to a lost cause. *Waverley* shows war in all its bearings, its large cultural implications, its splendour, its absurdity, its sadness. It has a unique place in our literature because it combines the keenest analytical intelligence with the sympathetic presentation of all the feelings aroused by war.

2 *Old Mortality*

In British religious and political history all roads lead back to the Civil War. Scott chose not to go back so far, but to pause in the year 1679, and distil the essence of great events out of the limited action of the Lowland revolt against the Stuarts. The public events treated in *Old Mortality* occupy about four pages in chapter 67 of the standard seventeenth century of Scott's time, that of David Hume. The wider English scene could be ruled out, as it could not in the Jacobite novels. England in *Old Mortality* is only the distant source of the severe instructions of Claverhouse's army. The necessary public events being few and simple, Scott was able to concentrate more intensely than anywhere else in his work on one of the deepest formative influences on the Scotland he knew, the zeal of the Covenanters. Here is the high moment of the tradition which was to become for Davie Deans in *The Heart of Midlothian* a nostalgic memory of the true heroism which, after two more generations, seemed almost to have faded from the earth. Yet it is one of Scott's key points that people seldom live in the present. Major Allan remembers Dunbar, and Bothwell refers to Old Noll. In the same way, Scott, like a man casting his eye over a wide landscape, and gradually moving from one landmark to another until he gains the far distance, Scott is able to travel nearly one hundred and forty years. This is the furthest possible reach of the collector of oral traditions. The essential link is Old Mortality himself, the keeper of the gravestones; and he is quite different from all the tedious land-lords, grandfathers and schoolmasters, who introduce so many of his books. As the guardian of the graves he is the guardian of the tradition.

A civilized tradition needs a form; it is experienced through habitual acts, whether ritual or merely customary. Here the covenanting tradition was especially vulnerable. It was a tradition that needed to be experienced at its highest pitch, in battle, in preaching, in martyrdom. In the narra-tive of *Old Mortality*, we see all these in their grandeur and misery. But we miss the flavour of Scott's mind, of his long, melancholy perspectives, if we are not always aware of the presence of Old Mortality tending the gravestones, and be-hind him yet another much less dramatic figure, Pattieson the schoolmaster.

Like many men who are powerless to preserve a beloved tradition, Old Mortality almost exults in its decay: "*We* are the only true Whigs. Carnal men have assumed that triumphant appellation, following him whose kingdom is of this world. Which of them would sit six hours on a wet hill-side to hear a godly sermon? I trow an hour o't wad staw them. They are ne'er a hair better than them that shamena to take upon themsells the persecuting name of bluidthirsty Tories."[1] Pattieson cannot even feel this passionate regret. His life is monotonous and melancholy, its worst trouble the indiscipline of his pupils, its sweetest hours spent in solitary walks. He is the passive witness of the death of tradition, signalized by the death of Old Mortality himself: "The com-mon people still regard his memory with great respect; and many are of opinion that the stones which he repaired will not again require the assistance of the chisel. They even assert that on the tombs where the manner of the martyrs' murder is recorded, their names have remained indelibly

[1] Chap i.

legible since the death of Old Mortality, while those of the persecutors, sculptured on the same monuments, have been entirely defaced. It is hardly necessary to say that this is a fond imagination, and that, since the time of the pious pilgrim, the monuments which were the objects of his care are hastening, like all earthly memorials, into ruin or decay.''[1]

This is a key passage, and he who fully understands it has grasped some of the essential features of Scott's mind. First, there is the enjoyment of the rich, imaginative treatment of the commonplace. Less fancifully than Sir Thomas Browne, more sympathetically than Hume and Gibbon he applies to the given context the general and just conclusion. Scott does not dwell, as Browne would have done, on the implied relation between gravestones and the living memory of the dead. But he altogether avoids the enlightened and progressive sneer that Gibbon, and perhaps Hume, would have given. Nevertheless, the passage contains irony, just as theirs would have done; but the irony is inherent in the situation and not applied. No turn of phrase draws attention to it. The irony is that the legend of the opposite treatment accorded by time and decay to the sculptured names of heroes and villains could only have grown up among people who never went to see. They never went to see because they had lost interest. Therefore, their legend was a survival, a superstition, even an unconscious excuse for no longer caring. The true tradition has died with Old Mortality; the spiritual as well as the material monuments are indeed 'hastening into ruin.'

One wonders how many of those who have so warmly praised the irony of Gibbon have missed the subtler irony here. In part the difference is one of temperament, a function of Scott's geniality and modesty against Gibbon's conscious

[1] Chap 1.

superiority. But the difference goes deeper. Unlike Gibbon, Scott has no final standard of historical judgment. So he has not the ultimate confidence that would have induced Gibbon to say according to his view of the forgotten dead, either 'their degenerate successors' or 'the more worldly judgment of a less zealous but more rational age'. For Scott each stage of civilization is valid in itself but relative as compared with others. The irony is, as it were, self-inflicted by his characters. In part, we know, Scott possessed the civilized, rational eighteenth century mind. But because this was always at war with other facets of his thought, the Gibbonian certainty issuing in the Gibbonian irony has gone.

Hume is more sceptical than Gibbon, but because he wrote about English history, because of his intellectual superiority to almost all his rival historians, he is more important for our purpose. Indeed, I doubt whether Scott's aims or his achievements in uniting the seventeenth century can be fully understood without reading him. And the key point here is Hume's use of the word 'fanatic', which he applies explicitly to Cromwell, and would have happily applied to almost all the rebels in *Old Mortality*. It is important to remember that 'everybody' read Hume, and down to the time of Carlyle at least, most people agreed with him.

Now the striking thing about Hume's use of the word 'fanatic' is that it invariably signals a fixed judgment and a closed question. When we think of the humane, flexible and moderate tone of Hume's account of the struggles of the seventeenth century, the guarded and balanced style of his apologia for the Stuarts, this rigidity of judgment comes as a surprise. Among other things, Scott in *Old Mortality* was reopening the supposedly closed question, 'What is fanaticism?'

It may be thought that I have come near to contradicting myself by saying that the death of Old Mortality is the end of a tradition, and at the same time describing the zeal of the

Covenanters as a formative influence on the Scotland of Scott's own time. But that is precisely the point. Scott shows us that the true covenanting zeal, depending on a state of continuous mental excitement, thrives only in times of crisis. He shows that Balfour is driven always to intensify his passion until madness overtakes him; those whose zeal is less decline into respectability and imagine that they perform their duty to the great tradition by merely repeating idle tales about the gravestones they never bother to see. Such, as Scott sees it, is the nemesis of the tradition which lacks the necessary features of tradition, ceremony, custom, a body of agreed assumptions.

Then, in opposition to Hume, and to general Augustan assumptions, he shows that fanaticism can also exist on the conservative side of the question, and then shows the different development of the two traditions in succeeding generations. Thus, Claverhouse, like Balfour, is a fanatic. But in quieter times his successors can decline into men of 'enjoying temper' (a phrase used by Bagehot[1] of Scott himself), who respect custom and guide their lives by tradition. But the Whig[2] tradition will go sour. Secretly ashamed of not having the zeal of their heroic ancestors, the eighteenth century Lowlanders will decline into sharp, canting money-grubbers, like the blacksmith, who "as he was a professor, would drive a nail for no man on the Sabbath, or kirk-fast, unless it were a case of absolute necessity, for which he always charged sixpence each shoe."[3] In a case like that, one can fairly say that the tradition is essentially dead, but that it is still a formative influence.

[1] See Bagehot: *Estimations in Criticism.* Ed Cuthbert Lennox. 1919 vol II.
[2] The word *Whig* is used here to refer to the Lowland Scots opposed to the King and the Anglican Church. Memories of Lord John Russell are not helpful here.
[3] *Waverley* chap 30.

Hume was one of those immensely persuasive men who employ brilliant intellectual powers in simplifying. Thus the simple antithesis of the 'fanatic' or 'enthusiast' (the covenanting type) and the 'superstitious' (the royalist Anglican) satisfies him. Those who are not covered by either term are simply selfish men without principle, like the hypocritical blacksmith, on one side, or violent, sensual men like Bothwell on the other. Scott is intent on showing how much more complex these psychological questions really are.

The first and most obvious contrast in *Old Mortality* is that between Balfour and Bothwell, whose two meetings need to be compared to be fully understood. We meet Bothwell in chapter 4, and learn of his poverty, his fecklessness and his royal descent. We find, too, that though he represents the forces of order, he is himself oppressive, lawless and undisciplined. Only when the officer is called away does he impertinently seize the opportunity to force the company to drink the health of the Archbishop of St. Andrews. It is characteristic of Bothwell to demand this tribute to religion and established order in a tone which conveys a sneer at the solemnity of the Covenanters' preaching style and, by implication, at all serious piety:

"I make so bold as to request of your precision, beloved, that you will arise from your seat, beloved, and having bent your hams until your knees do rest upon the floor, beloved, that you will turn over this measure (called by the profane a gill) of the comfortable creature brandy, to the health and glorification of his Grace the Archbishop of St. Andrews."

Balfour, glaring ferociously, asks what will be the consequence if he refuses, and is told in the same tone of insulting parody that his nose will be pulled and he will be beaten with the flat of the sword. Balfour's response is surprising:

"Is it even so? then give me the cup; The Archbishop of St. Andrews, and the place he now worthily holds;—may each prelate in Scotland soon be as the Right Reverend James Sharpe!"[1]

As the reader will soon learn that Balfour has taken part in the murder of the Archbishop, so recently that even the fact of his death is not yet known to the company, this is intensely dramatic. But it is more; it is one of the most telling strokes in Scott's patiently constructed psychological portrait of the 'enthusiastic' mentality. An ordinary man would be afraid of the soldiers and accept the cup. A very brave man would stand by his principles and refuse to submit to intimidation. Balfour's courage is unquestionable. But such a course is not startling and dangerous enough for him. He must create drama, he must take a risk that the present situation, formidable as it is, does not require of him. He must pursue his dead enemy with irony, in a way which is likely, later on, to be interpreted as a confession or rather a boast of guilt. Why this foolhardiness? Balfour, though extremely brave, is not as a rule foolhardy. A little later he shelters from the pursuit of the soldiers in the outhouses of Morton's uncle. But he is reckless of consequences here because he conceives himself to be conveying the divine irony, the irony of history itself.

There follows a wrestling-match in which Bothwell is thrown, a foretaste of the second scene between the two at the battle of Drumclog. It is characteristic of Scott's technique, when, as here, he is writing at his best, to make a single device achieve several results. There is not only the dramatic exchange of these two antitypes, there is also the onlooker who is Morton the hero. When Bothwell is thrown one of his fellow-soldiers draws his sword and threatens the victor. Here Morton's natural sense of moderation and fair play, so strongly in contrast with each of the others, causes him to intervene with the words: "Stand back! it was all

[1] Chap 4.

fair play; your comrade sought a fall, and he has got it."
So it is that Morton, through his sense of fair play, first
moves into the orbit of his evil genius, Balfour. But men like
Bothwell, however oppressive they may be, have a code,
the traditional military and manly code. They have the
illusion despite much evidence that the seriousness and religious intensity of the Lowland Whigs are a cloak for cowardice and hypocrisy.[1] Bothwell's support of the Church and the
Archbishop is accidental, a mere corollary of the military
position in which he finds himself. His respect for a man who
can beat him in a fair wrestling-match is genuine, an expression of his deepest feelings. So he does not allow his
fellow-soldier to interfere and says: "I did not think there
was a crop-ear of them all could have laid the best cap and
feather in the King's Life-Guards on the floor of a rascally
change-house. Hark ye, friend, give me your hand." Respect is not mutual. To Balfour the courage which he himself and Bothwell share is nothing unless sanctified by faith
and a good cause. Bothwell has lost more than a fall at
wrestling. He has been forced to respect a despised enemy,
and worse still, he has been forced to respect a man who
despises him. We begin to see how it is that Scott will make
the defeat of the royal forces at the minor skirmish of Drumclog into an event in some ways more significant than their
decisive victory at Bothwell Brig. This is the extra di-
mension in Scott's view of history that Hume could not have
understood. You cannot judge by results.

It is at Drumclog that Bothwell and Balfour meet again
and recognize each other, and the words of each are true to

[1] Thus at Claverhouse's council before the battle of Drumclog:
" 'Pshaw!' said the young Cornet, 'what signifies strong ground,
when it is only held by a crew of canting psalm-singing old
women?' 'A man may fight never the worse,' retorted Major
Allan, 'for honouring both his Bible and his Psalter.' " The Major
remembers Dunbar.

type: "Then a bed of heather or a thousand marks" says Bothwell. "The sword of the Lord and of Gideon", says Balfour. For one, luck is lord of the battlefield. For the other, war is only significant for its religious meaning.

When Balfour gets the better of Bothwell, and gives him his death-blow:

" 'Die, wretch! die!' said Balfour, redoubling the thrust with better aim; and, setting his foot on Bothwell's body as he fell, he a third time transfixed him with his sword. —'Die, bloodthirsty dog! die as thou hast lived! die, like the beasts that perish—hoping nothing—believing nothing——'

'And *fearing* nothing!' said Bothwell, collecting the last effort of respiration to utter these desperate words, and expiring as soon as they were spoken."

Those last three words of Bothwell should be taken together with Claverhouse's comment that follows: "The king has lost a servant and the devil has got one."[1]

The contrast here is very characteristic of Scott's mind. He has shown the general worthlessness of Bothwell, how the only pride of his life is his royal blood, his only aim to enjoy the pleasures of the camp, but he must also show this low-minded version of military honour at its highest point, its insensate courage in death. But from another view this highest point is also the lowest point; it implies desperate contempt for the soul and its immortality (neglected by many in the book but doubted by none); and so comes Claverhouse's flat comment, which takes up and enforces for the reader this second meaning of Bothwell's words, which might be momentarily overlooked in the excitement of the drama of his human courage and defiance of Balfour. Bothwell means that he does not fear hell, as well as meaning that he does not fear pain and death.

But this contrast does not exhaust the matter; for Claver-

[1] Chap 16.

house is not a chorus, but an active participant, who must also come under the lens of the author's enquiry. The historical Claverhouse was a great royalist hero, whom Scott admired very much as his letters show. Scott does not gloss over his severity. But he sees beyond the distinction of parties, and shows us that in his ultimate essence he is really much more like Balfour than he is like Bothwell. This surprising similarity is part of Scott's strategy from the first, but we become aware of it only gradually, and perhaps the passage just quoted is the first hint. How like, and yet how unlike, is Claverhouse's comment on the dead or dying Bothwell to Balfour's. It is like in that it embodies the same judgment. Bothwell is a man without spiritual significance, just a useful soldier and nothing more. And yet, this unquestionable similarity of judgment somehow seems misleading. Why? Because the tone of the two statements is utterly different. Balfour speaks as if claiming to be the appointed deputy of the Lord, Claverhouse cynically, and with an affectation of indifference. There is a puzzle here which Scott has in reserve; there is no time to unravel it in the midst of one of the most exciting scenes of action to be found in his works. He returns to it much later, in a quiet passage when Morton is Claverhouse's prisoner, after being saved from imminent death at the hands of the Covenanters.

Then we see Claverhouse giving orders for life and death:

"All these various orders,—for life and death, the securing of his prisoners, and the washing his charger's shoulder,— were given in the same unmoved and equable voice, . . .

The Cameronians, so lately about to be the willing agents of a bloody execution, were now themselves to undergo it. They seemed prepared alike for either extremity, nor did any of them show the least sign of fear."[1]

The similarity between Claverhouse and the Covenanters

[1] Chap 34.

lies in courage based not only on devotion to the cause but on fatalism. But, of course, Claverhouse's fatalism is secular, that of the Covenanters is based on, or at least justified by, the Calvinist doctrine of predestination.

How much difference does this make? This is a question of great complexity and general importance, which Scott was unusually well-equipped to answer. It is hard to imagine a more serious question that a novel could pose. If there are any who still doubt the seriousness of Scott's aims as an artist, because they are dazzled by the tricks of the master-entertainer, and the devotion of long-past generations of boys, it is at points like this that conviction may come to them.

Claverhouse has his own version of the answer. When Morton hints at a similarity between him and Balfour, he replies:

"You are right, you are very right—we are both fanatics; but there is some distinction between the fanaticism of honour and that of dark and sullen superstition." And, when challenged with their likeness in shedding blood without mercy or remorse, goes on: "Surely, but of what kind?— There is a difference, I trust, between the blood of learned and reverend prelates and scholars, of gallant soldiers and noble gentlemen, and the red puddle that stagnates in the veins of psalm-singing mechanics, crack-brained demagogues, and sullen boors;—some distinction, in short, between spilling a flask of generous wine, and dashing down a can of base muddy ale?"[1] Morton's reply is damning and conclusive: "Your distinction is too nice for my comprehension. God gives every spark of life—that of the peasant as well as of the prince;"

Scott here puts his finger on the difference between the worldly and the unworldly fatalism. Worldly fatalism must

[1] Chap 35.

rest in the end on the equation of power and justice. If Claverhouse is a highly intelligent, and in some respects sensitive and agreeable man, as Scott shows that he is, this is the consequence of natural gifts of personality developed by education. But behind it all lies the undiscriminating mind of the secular fatalist. It is not that he is too stupid to see the obvious objection, that the psalms, of which he speaks so contemptuously, are part of the agreed traditions of those learned prelates whom he claims to defend. For the prelates, too, of course, are seen in purely secular terms, as upholders of the established order. Love of war is the active, class-conservatism the passive side of the secular fatalism.

Endlessly fair and patient, Scott is not deterred by the clearness with which he sees all this from giving the romance of military glory its full weight and dignity, when Claverhouse says:

"It is not the expiring pang that is worth thinking of in an event that must happen one day, and may befall us on any given moment—it is the memory which the soldier leaves behind him, like the long train of light that follows the sunken sun—that is all which is worth caring for, which distinguishes the death of the brave or the ignoble. When I think of death, Mr. Morton, as a thing worth thinking of, it is in the hope of pressing one day some well-fought and hard-won field of battle, and dying with the shout of victory in my ear—*that* would be worth dying for, and more, it would be worth having lived for!"[1]

Weight and dignity, yes; but futility also. The secular fatalism is bold and graceful, but leads in the end to despair. For the cause is not worth the sacrifice, since it is not truly believed in as a cause, but only as a choice of loyalties. It is nearer to support of the home side in sport than to the devotion of the Covenanters.

[1] Chap 34.

So far I have been speaking, in the interests of clearness and simplicity of 'the Covenanters'. But the variations among them are many and subtle. Scott shows us that the religious fatalism, being the expression of profounder ideas and stronger feelings than are possessed by Bothwell or Claverhouse, is capable of attaining a higher heroism or a deeper degradation.

Balfour suffers in our estimation when compared with Claverhouse, and the reason for this is interesting. Balfour, as we have seen, has a great religious tradition behind him; Claverhouse has only the courage of a soldier and the loyalties of a gentleman. Balfour is just as brave and resourceful, just as intelligent. But Scott shows that both men are by nature worldly, and somewhat self-centred. This temperament can fit lightly and easily into the royalist and gentlemanly loyalties. There is no unbearable tension in Claverhouse's mind. When defeated at Drumclog, he takes it as part of the game. Balfour is constantly trying to force his selfish purposes into the unyielding mould of the covenanting doctrine. But strong natures like his do not take kindly to hypocrisy. So he has moments of terrible sincerity, when the muffled doubts become audible. So he says to Morton:

" 'Young man, you are already weary of me, and would be yet more so, perchance, did you know the task upon which I have been lately put. [He is referring to the murder of the Archbishop.] And I wonder not that it should be so, for there are times when I am weary of myself. Think you not it is a sore trial for flesh and blood, to be called upon to execute the righteous judgments of Heaven while we are yet in the body, and continue to retain that blinded sense and sympathy for carnal suffering which makes our own flesh thrill when we strike a gash upon the body of another! And think you that when some prime tyrant has been removed from his place, that the instruments of his punishment can at all times look back on their share in his downfall with firm and unshaken nerves? Must they not sometimes even question the truth of that inspiration which they have felt and acted under?"[1]

It would be impossible to overrate the terror of this last question for a man like Balfour. Morton's reply brings no comfort:

" 'I own I should strongly doubt the origin of any inspiration which seemed to dictate a line of conduct contrary to those feelings of natural humanity, which Heaven has assigned to us as the general law of our conduct.' "

It is a pity that these words are phrased in the remote and abstract style that is so often employed by Scott's heroes. But this should not prevent us from seeing the seriousness of the issue raised. Moreover, it is not just an interesting philosophical bypath; it is making explicit something which is inherent in the whole action of the novel. It helps us to understand Balfour's strange but perfectly consistent career. The covenanting religion rests everything on twin foundations of authority and experience. The authority is God's voice in Scripture to which the passionate experience of the converted soul responds. Not only, as we have seen, are ceremony, custom, tradition rejected, but so are reason and conscience. Or rather, conscience is not exactly rejected but transformed into direct inspiration. There is no such thing, then, as morality; no rational enquiry into conduct remains possible. There is only obedience or disobedience to the Divine *fiat*. This can indeed be sought in Scripture, but as Scripture is difficult and multifarious, Divine inspiration is required to choose the passage of Scripture which will decide the question. Hence Balfour's talk of being zealous unto slaying, when his passions or policy are determined on violence, but never a word of other texts that speak of forgiveness. But Balfour, as we have seen, is the impure fanatic, his

[1] Chap 6.

mind clouded with selfish desires. We shall see later the consequences of this doctrine of Divine inspiration in the case of a selfless fanatic, Macbriar.

To question the truth of the inspiration, therefore, is for Balfour to make a breach in the one barrier against the abyss of despair. The only refuge is a complete suppression of doubt. But Balfour's mind is too direct and forceful for this. So, as he cannot retreat into a more conventional view of conduct, as he cannot abandon the terrible progression of his bloodthirsty acts, there is no escape for him. The tension must increase, outward fanaticism must grow greater as doubts multiply, and he must go mad. Melodramatic and unconvincing Morton's last meeting with him may be but Balfour's psychological development is grasped and presented with perfect clearness.

Fanaticism is a solemn and terrible subject; and it is characteristic of Scott to give it its full dignity where Hume and Gibbon had sneered. But this dignity does not exclude comedy; and the comedy that springs out of fanaticism is Scott's humour at its best. Though a very clever man, Scott was not, in any marked degree, witty. His letters contain few memorable phrases; and in the novels much of the humour is of the insipid, anecdotal quality of the ordinary shrewd man of the world. But there are occasions, and one of them is in chapter 8 of *Old Mortality*, when his sense of the seriousness of the moral substance of the personal life and his melancholy awareness of the pressure of events combine to produce comedy of the highest order.

Mause Headrigg and her son Cuddie have taken refuge in the house of Morton's uncle, an avaricious, peace-loving man, who attends the assembly of the 'indulged' presbyterian clergy, opposed to the Covenanters and passively loyal to the crown. Cuddie has an outlook very similar to old Morton's, though with an extra touch of peasant shrewdness and force.

" 'And now we're settled ance mair,' said Cuddie to his

THE ACHIEVEMENT OF WALTER SCOTT: PART II

mother, 'and if we're no sae bien and comfortable as we were
up yonder, yet life's life ony gate, and we're wi' decent kirk-
ganging folk o' your ain persuasion, mither; there will be nae
quarrelling about that.'

'Of *my* persuasion, hinnie!' said the too-enlightened Mause,
'wae's me for thy blindness and theirs. O, Cuddie, they are
but in the court of the Gentiles, and will ne'er win farther
ben, I doubt; they are but little better than the prelatists
themsells. They wait on the ministry of that blinded man,
Peter Poundtext, ance a precious teacher of the Word, but
now a backsliding pastor that has, for the sake of stipend and
family maintenance, forsaken the strict path, and gane
astray after the Black Indulgence.' "[1]

Not long after, a party of the King's troops, headed by
Bothwell, intimidate old Morton, and begin to make free
with the wine. Here Scott's ordinary humour is at work,
showing the miserly old man driven to be generous by the
master-passion of fear. This is acceptable as being psycho-
logically just, but is only mildly amusing. From this basis a
finely modulated chapter rises to the heights.

Cuddie pretends that his mother is deaf, and offers to
take her place in the test-ceremony of drinking the King's
health.

" 'Do you renounce the Covenant, good woman?' (Bothwell asks).

'Whilk Covenant is your honour meaning? Is it the
Covenant of Works, or the Covenant of Grace?' said Cuddie,
interposing.

'Any covenant; all covenants that ever were hatched,'
answered the trooper.

'Mither,' cried Cuddie, affecting to speak as to a deaf
person, 'the gentleman wants to ken if ye will renounce the
Covenant of Works?'

[1] Chap 8.

'With all my heart, Cuddie' said Mause, 'and pray that my feet may delivered from the snare thereof.'

'Come,' said Bothwell, 'the old dame has come more frankly off than I expected.' "

This is not only extraordinarily economical, it is, as very few comic passages are, profoundly revealing. To Mause the Covenant of Works is the Arminian or Catholic doctrine of salvation by works as well as faith. It denies total depravity, irresistible grace and all the glory and terror of the Calvinist tradition. She could not express her sense of the magnitude of the contrast between this and the true Covenant of God with his people. Cuddie knows her feeling well enough to play on it and deceive Bothwell, but cannot grasp its seriousness for her; still less has he an inkling of its dignity for us. For Bothwell 'covenant' is no more than a word used as a badge. That it really contains meaning, still more that it may contain a variety of meanings, according as it is used, is entirely beyond his comprehension. The comedy reflects dignity only on Mause, and casts the stigma of brutal, unthinking oppression upon Bothwell.

Comedy of this type might be called the opposite of Gibbon's witty passages about the homoiousion and the homoousion.[1] Once again, we see Scott going beyond and behind the classic Augustan statements about theological fanaticism, recovering the human content of formulae supposed to be dead. He makes Gibbon's sneer look cheap while never forgetting for a moment that he is writing as a novelist, not as a critic and commentator. The scene is brief, amusing, exciting, and perfectly in harmony with the logic of the whole situation.

But the chapter does not end here. Next Henry Morton is

---

[1] cf. *Decline and Fall* chap 21. "The profane of every age have derided the furious contests which the difference of a single diphthong excited."

questioned about his sheltering Balfour after the murder of the Archbishop. His uncle becomes more and more frightened. At last, all Cuddie's sly precaution is in vain, and Mause breaks out in full denunciation of the 'compliers and carnal self-seekers' with all her battery of references and quotations from the Old Testament. Old Morton, the other servants and her son tremble for the consequences. But Bothwell is only amused, for deep-rooted in his military code is the assumption that the opinions of women cannot be taken seriously, and that those that are not sexually desirable must be treated with a rough respect. So the soldiers depart, taking Henry Morton under arrest on suspicion of abetting the murderer Balfour, and the chapter ends with a skilful anti-climax:

" 'Sae, come awa, come awa; the family hae had enough o' your testimony to mind it for ae while.'

So saying he dragged off Mause, the words, 'Testimony —Covenant—malignants—indulgence,' still thrilling upon her tongue, to make preparation for instantly renewing their travels in quest of an asylum. [Old Morton will, of course, now timidly cast them out.]

'Ill-faur'd, crazy, crack-brained gowk, that she is!' exclaimed the housekeeper, as she saw them depart, 'to set up to be sae muckle better than ither folk, the auld besom, and to bring sae muckle distress on a douce quiet family.' "

Scott knows how to place his great moments in the context of the ordinary; and he was determined to portray fanaticism in the round, in all kinds of circumstances, and affecting all kind of characters. Thus there is the fanaticism of pure endurance, represented by the old woman at the crossroads in chapter 5,[1] who sits hour after hour waiting

---

[1] She appears again years later, when Morton returns from abroad, and finds her still an unchanging example of endurance. See chap 52.

to direct 'our puir scattered remnant . . . before they fell into the nets of the oppressors.' Here the language of Balfour's party is transformed into a spirit of pure charity and self-sacrifice. Then the preacher Kettledrummle is utterly different again; he is the weak man with the gift of the gab and little power of thought, who in a secular age would make a political agitator. There is an amusing scene in chapter 14 where he and Mause interrupt each other with denunciations of their royalist captors. Bothwell, and in a later chapter Claverhouse, treat this as of no more significance than the buzzing of flies. The currency has been devalued; and we have the first hint of what we will see clearly in Scott's account of the eighteenth century in other books. The great affirmations of the Covenanters' creed can be transformed into cant.

After the victory at Drumclog men like Kettledrummle come into their own: "The discourse which he pronounced . . . was divided into fifteen heads, each of which was gathered with seven uses of application, two of consolation, two of terror, two declaring the causes of backsliding and of wrath, and one announcing the promised and expected deliverance."[1]

But he is succeeded in the preaching by Macbriar, a true enthusiast, for whom the cause annihilates all thought of self. His sermon which is too long to quote should be read entire as one of the finest imaginative recreations of a whole school of eloquence.

The time must come when the pure and the impure fanaticism will clash; it comes when Balfour is trying to keep the doubtful adherence of Morton to the cause by the use of political arguments which the Covenanters denominate 'carnal reason'.

" 'Peace, Ephraim Macbriar!' again interrupted Burley.

[1] Chap 18.

'I will not peace', said the young man. 'Is it not the cause of my Master who hath sent me? Is it not a profane and Erastian destroying of His authority, usurpation of His power, denial of His name to place either King or Parliament in His place as the master and governor of His household, the adulterous husband of His spouse?'

'You speak well,' said Burley, dragging him aside, 'but not wisely; your own ears have heard this night in council how this scattered remnant are broken and divided, and would ye now make a veil of separation between them?' "[1]

Here is the tragedy of the high cause in the workaday world, isolated and analysed here perhaps for the first time in the English novel. George Eliot would later transpose it with great subtlety into professional and scholarly terms in *Middlemarch*. It is the privilege of the pioneer to be excelled, and George Eliot's treatment is more profound. But credit as high or higher is due to Scott, who was the first to break through the wall of incomprehension erected by Hume, and the other philosophic historians. Scott was the first to see that each in his own way Balfour (here called Burley) and Macbriar are both right, that each has an unanswerable point against the other, that the weakness of each opposing view is inherent in the conditions of life itself, that 'hypocrisy' is no explanation but a lazy refusal to examine the matter closely.

But even Macbriar is not fanaticism's highest point. Reading about the Covenanters is like climbing a series of false summits, as in Pope's description of learning.[2] There is a more terrible figure than Macbriar, so terrible that even Macbriar feels the impulse to sooth and restrain him. Mucklewrath speaks like this:

" 'Who speaks of mercy to the bloody house of the malignants? I say take the infants and dash them against the

[1] Chap 21.   [2] *Essay on Criticism* ll. 215-232.

148

stones; take the daughters and mothers of the house and hurl them from the battlements of their trust, that the dogs may fatten on their blood as they did on that of Jezebel, the spouse of Ahab, and that their carcasses may be dung to the face of the field even in their portion of their fathers.' "

It is notable that all the preachers from the most moderate to the most violent use biblical illustrations. Such, the book suggests, is the nemesis of biblical literalism. What is theoretically the most rigid system is in reality the most individualist. Almost any moral doctrine or practical conclusion can be extracted from the sacred text, when the most eccentric interpretations are permitted. Whatever personal passion or quirk of thought is being justified, the conclusion can be presented as given by Divine authority. The unwary might be tempted to think that these differences are no more than a matter of degree of vehemence. But having shown these differences of tone and language, Scott has the consequence in reserve. Chapter 33 shows the immense practical importance of those differences of theological tone that the writers of the enlightenment had dismissed as trivial.

Morton, wrongly suspected of having betrayed the covenanting cause at the disastrous defeat of Bothwell Brig, stumbles by accident into the place of greatest danger during the general flight. He finds himself in a room where all the leading preachers are met together. Mucklewrath characteristically sees a sign:

" 'We have prayed, and wrestled and petitioned for an offering to atone the sins of the congregation, and lo! the very head of the offence is delivered into our hand. He hath burst in like a thief through the window; he is a ram caught in the thicket, whose blood shall be a drink-offering to redeem vengeance from the church, and the place shall from henceforth be called Jehovah-Jireh, for the sacrifice is provided. Up then, and bind the victim with cords to the horns of the altar!' "

Here is the crucial test of the most extreme form of covenanting biblical interpretation. What has really happened?
A man, suspected of treachery, has come into a room unexpectedly. A thousand passages in the Bible of differing
import could be used as parallels. The mind of Mucklewrath
seizes on the one that fulfils his animosity. Macbriar pleads
for a fair hearing, though without disputing that if he has
indeed betrayed the cause he must be put to death. And even
he, when he finds Morton's defence unconvincing, says: 'We
are not free to let you pass from us safe and in life, since
Providence hath given you into our hands at the moment
when we prayed with godly Joshua, saying, "What shall we
say when Israel turneth their backs before their enemies?"
Then camest thou, delivered to us as it were by lot, that thou
mightest sustain the punishment . . .'

But it is Sunday evening, and Macbriar says that they will
not spill blood on the Sabbath. They wait, intending to put
him to death when midnight strikes. But Mucklewrath cannot wait:

" 'As the sun went back on the dial ten degrees for inti-
mating the recovery of holy Hezekiah, so shall it now go forward, that the wicked may be taken away from among the
people, and the Covenant established in its purity.' " With
this he begins to move the hands of the clock forward, and
prepare for the killing, when a moment later Morton is
saved by Claverhouse's men.

This scene is difficult, and worth very careful attention.
There are three rules of conduct at work here. There are
ordinary instincts of humanity, which would lead people of
normal sensibility to spare Morton. This is the code of conduct that Macbriar calls 'carnal reluctance to see his blood
spilt'. He may be called fanatical and inhuman, but speaks
entirely in accord with the logic of the Calvinist position,
which the Covenanters have taken up. For their cardinal
principle is that grace and nature are eternal opposites. All

natural instincts are bad, therefore a true Covenanter ought
to take no more notice of his impulse to mercy in such a case
than a brave soldier would take of the natural human impulse to flinch in battle. Then the idea of refraining from
blood on the Sabbath, which is Macbriar's, is *not*, 'Do not let
us do evil on the Lord's day', but, 'Do not let us do the
Lord's work on the divinely appointed day of rest.'

But Mucklewrath's outlook is entirely different again. It
would be a complete mistake to regard his action in moving
the hands of the clock as a trick or a deceit. He believes himself to be performing a miracle as the words he uses to justify
the action show. One cannot feel the strangeness and solemnity of his act without entering imaginatively into the intensity of his belief in the inviolable Sabbath. To suspend the
binding force of an absolute Divine command is a moral
miracle. Mucklewrath here stands as far from the normal
covenanting outlook as the other Covenanters are from
'carnal' morality. Thus it is in full earnest, and not with the
loose superiority of the enlightenment that Scott here calls
Mucklewrath a 'maniac'—a term he would never have used
of Macbriar. And so with these five beautifully contrasted
figures, so different in their superficial similarity, Scott com-
pletes his profound analysis of the idea, previously supposed
so simple, of religious enthusiasm. Balfour, Kettledrummle,
Macbriar, Mucklewrath, and the unnamed old woman at
the crossing are all different and all in the end are understood in their human fullness.

3 *Rob Roy*

Rob Roy is a difficult book to put in perspective. It is undoubtedly a work of distinction, and very characteristic of
its author. It is not marred by the facility which makes
several of the works of Scott's middle period (*Woodstock*, for
instance) into agreeable adventure stories with just a touch
or two of the master's hand. On the contrary, it is carefully
planned and highly intelligent. There is charm in some of the
early chapters, and excitement in some of the later ones. Yet
it cannot be called a major work of art in the sense in which
Waverley and *Old Mortality* are.

In its imagined chronology it falls neatly half-way between
these two masterpieces. It deals with 1715, as they cover
1679 and 1745. Now it was likely, in any event, that a man
so deeply interested in Jacobite history as Scott should deal
at some time with the events of 1715. But we must always remember the almost incredible speed with which Scott produced his earliest and best books. In three years he published,
besides various minor works, *Waverley*, *Guy Mannering*, *The
Antiquary*, *The Black Dwarf*, *Old Mortality* and *Rob Roy*. We
always have to reckon with Scott's superhuman energy, but
this was a special case. For in their general outline and meaning the events of 1715 and 1745 are curiously alike. One has
the sensation in reading the accounts of the two risings of a
moment of history congealed and repeated; military fortunes varied, of course, but parties, loyalties and arguments
were not greatly changed. Clearly for a writer of Scott's

152

method, so devoted as he was to oral traditions, the more recent of the two risings held greater advantages. So there was a danger that he would merely attempt to do *Waverley* over again. As *Waverley* was almost perfect, failure would have been inevitable. *Rob Roy* is not by any means *Waverley* over again, yet it feels its magnetic pull in a way that is damaging. It can be thought of as an anti-Waverley.[1] Summarize its conclusions, and this is approximately the answer you get. Yet in its method and narrative line, it is curiously different. Where the plot of *Waverley* is a perfect symbolic expression of its meaning, the plot of *Rob Roy* is perfunctory. The 1715 rebellion is hustled in at the end almost apologetically. The line of causation in a succession of events, always, as we have seen,[2] one of Scott's strongest points when his mind is working strongly, is here blurred, and even contains touches of absurdity. It is not merely impossible to take Rashleigh Osbaldistone seriously as a psychological study; it is very difficult to make sense of the motives of his villainy even at the detective story level. There can be few feebler connections made in the whole of Scott's work than that between Rashleigh's plot and the Jacobite rising:

" 'You think, then,' said I . . . 'that Rashleigh Osbaldistone has done this injury to my father, merely to accelerate a rising in the Highlands, by distressing the gentlemen to whom the bills were originally granted.' "[3]

In the last chapters old Sir Hildebrand's sons disappear like a mist; yet in the early chapters they are depicted with some care, and with a broad humorous skill.

This curious sense of unreality in the later chapters when the Osbaldistones of Northumberland are swept away should be carefully distinguished from the breakdown of plot

---

[1] The discussion of this question by Professor Donald Davie is of interest. See his *The Heyday of Walter Scott* chap 5.
[2] See chap 4, above. Part I   [3] *Rob Roy* chap 26.

at the end of *Guy Mannering* discussed in chapter 2. There is no question here of a reaction towards common-sense-and-no-nonsense after a high romantic flight. The Osbaldistones have not at any stage come in for romantic treatment. There is no sign of the touch of nostalgia which one might expect to be mingled with the disapproval in a man of Scott's temperament as he wrote of the lost world of the sporting, drinking squires. The presentation of the family in the opening chapters is broad, solid, humorous and mildly satirical. The point is here that the plot is not really to be taken seriously at all. The book is more like a set of social pictures interwoven with meditations on value than a novel. This makes it a very strange production from the pen of the wizard of the north, the prince of storytellers. Few great writers reveal so little about their real aims and methods of work (as opposed to their sources) as Scott does. So there is no proper evidence about the reasons for this. But one may guess that is is here that what I have called the magnetic pull of *Waverley* is most felt. The plot of *Waverley* is a masterly interweaving of public and private events. The general similarity of the two risings inhibited an attempt at repetition.

But all the time, Scott was, of course, a natural storyteller. It would not have occurred to him to write a novel without a plot, a mere set of comparative social sketches, like, say Percy Lubbock's *Roman Pictures*. So, in a certain sense, there is still a good deal of plot in *Rob Roy*. But it is stagy, exaggerated, and perfunctory. What ought to be the key events are ridiculously compressed. Scott, the most sincere and honest of men, here sadly falls victim to a psychological law which can be studied in the utterances of politicians: if you are determined to carry out a policy, but do not really believe in it, you will defend it with extravagant gestures. The strong events in *Rob Roy* for the most part are like that. The currency of excitement is debased by Rashleigh's villainy or by the sudden deaths of his numerous brothers.

But what is alive and valuable in the book, (and that is still a great deal of it) has much more the character of a meditation, even of an introspective enquiry by the author into his own standards of judgment in the face of something which he had treated in masterly fashion in *Waverley*, but which could be examined in so many different ways. It was, of course, the clash of cultures, the struggle between the old world and the new which was embodied in the history of the Jacobite rebellions; and it fascinated him all his life.

The contrast between the treatment in *Waverley* and that in *Rob Roy* could be shown at many points. A particularly instructive one is to be found in the difference between Flora Mac-Ivor and Diana Vernon. At first sight, Flora seems the more outlandish, romanticized figure, as we glimpse her beauty by the Highland waterfalls, while Diana Vernon is comparatively domestic and credible. But this is quite misleading. Flora's romantic devotion to the Jacobite cause is perfectly placed and understood, and has a well-defined function in the plot because of her influence on her brother's calculating spirit. But Diana Vernon is seen just as the narrator sees her. It is perfectly natural and right that she should have charmed Victorian schoolboys. In a superficial sense she is perfectly life-like, saucy and high-spirited. In terms of the deeper artistic purposes for which Flora Mac-Ivor has her being, she simply does not exist.

It is often said that Scott's heroines are uninteresting and are just part of the machinery of his books. As a generalization this has enough rough justice to be accepted. But Diana Vernon really stands in a separate, intermediate position. A heroine like Edith Bellenden in *Old Mortality* has little relation to the book's central concerns. Flora Mac-Ivor is an essential part of *Waverley*'s whole structure. But Diana Vernon is a perfectly respectable day-dream of the not impossible she. The man who has such day-dreams is showing himself to be, as Scott was, a very decent, intelligent, observant and shrewd person. But he is not at all showing himself as what he also was, a great novelist.

Waverley, as we have seen, was not so much a study of the difference between Jacobites and Hanoverians as a study of different kinds of Jacobite. But inevitably a fair amount of comment on Hanoverian theories and behaviour comes in incidentally. One type of Hanoverian is treated with special contempt, and that is the type represented by Richard Waverley, the commercial type. Contempt for the commercial classes is a persistent tradition of English culture, aristocratic, professional and intellectual. Charlotte Yonge's horror of people 'in trade', Hardy comparing Browning to a dissenting grocer, and socialists of the present century are all following a venerable eighteenth century tradition, though their general opinions and motives may vary widely.

Now the treatment of Richard Waverley is not really unfair, for the spectacle of a man choosing his political loyalties in a time of great national upheaval by considerations of profit is unpleasing. But no one knew better than Scott that a soldier, who in one sense, is a professional killer, may be a gentle and humane man. Suppose, on the same analogy that a commercial man, professionally devoted to profit, could be unselfish and even generous. A great deal of English social history is contained in the fact that while the first idea about the soldier is part of our literary tradition and general background of ideas, the second is comparatively a stranger. By a curious but not altogether surprising paradox it was left to the great heroic novelist, the matchless celebrator of kings and heroes to redress the balance. It is not altogether surprising for two reasons. Scott would not have been the great heroic novelist he was if he had not possessed also some of the instincts of the shrewd Lowland Scots from whom he was descended. But the second point is more important still. It was in Scott's nature always to reconsider and often to amend any easy expressions of contempt he might have uttered in haste. He is one of the fairest of our great writers.

It will be obvious by now that I am maintaining that Bailie Nicol Jarvie, not Rob Roy himself, is the key figure of the book. But Scott's strategy in preparing for him is, characteristically, slow and deliberately deceptive. Except that he does it with more geniality, his method of laying a trap for the reader is almost like that of Swift.

At first the presentation of the narrator's father, William Osbaldistone does not seem so very different from that of Richard Waverley, while the general family situation is almost exactly repeated. In each case the young hero has a commercial Whig father and a landowning Jacobite uncle. William Osbaldistone certainly carries commercial enthusiasm to an extreme:

"He never used threats, or expressions of loud resentment. All was arranged with him on system, and it was his practice to do 'the needful' on every occasion without wasting words about it. It was, therefore, with a bitter smile that he listened to my imperfect answers concerning the state of commerce in France, and unmercifully permitted me to involve myself deeper and deeper in the mysteries of agio, tariffs, tare and tret; nor can I charge my memory with his having looked positively angry, until he found me unable to explain the exact effect which the depreciation of the louis d'or had produced on the negotiation of bills of exchange. 'The most remarkable national occurrence in my time' said my father (who nevertheless had seen the Revolution), 'and he knows no more of it than a post on the quay.' "[1]

A little later the head clerk says:

" 'Mr. Francis seems to understand the fundamental principle of all moral accounting, the great ethic rule of three. Let A do to B as he would have B do to him; the

[1] Chap 2.

product will give the rule of conduct required.' My father smiled. . . ."

The smile may contain a touch of saving grace, but we are not far here from the world of Dickens' Gradgrind, it seems.

William Osbaldistone never becomes, and is not meant to become, a very sympathetic figure. Yet there are enough hints to show that he has not entirely obliterated the sentiments of his aristocratic family in the pursuit of gain. It may be true that "to have proved him the lineal descendant of William the Conqueror would have far less flattered his vanity than the hum and bustle which his approach was wont to produce among the bulls, bears and brokers of Stock-Alley."[1] Nevertheless he has partly transferred the sensitive family pride to business, so that a strong hidden feeling bursts out momentarily when he rebukes the clerk, pleading for the recalcitrant heir: "Do you think I will ask him twice to be my friend, my assistant and my confidant? —to be a partner of my cares and of my fortune? Owen, I thought you had known me better."

We feel the force of this more strongly when we have been introduced to the other branch of the family. Young Frank approaches the home of his ancestors with eagerness stimulated both by the romantic tales told him by his nurse, and by his father's mysterious separation from his relatives. His disillusionment with the dull dissipation of the life of a sporting squire is extreme. He finds that there is no great distinction between devotion to the Jacobite cause, and the trade of the highwayman.

" A man in those days might have all the external appearance of a gentleman, and yet turn out to be a highwayman . . . the profession of the polite and accomplished adventurer, who nicked you out of your money at White's, or

[1] Chap 4.

bowled you out of it at Marybone, was often united with that
of the professed ruffian, who, on Bagshot Heath, or Finchley
Common, commanded his brother beau to stand and deliver."[1] Passages like this, following so soon after the account
of Frank's commercial father, alter the perspective. Who are
the money-grubbers now? The aristocratic distaste for trade
ceases to appear as a noble superiority, and becomes more
like the voice of hypocritical idleness. The words omitted in
the passage quoted just now are of particular interest, and
show how in the midst of his melodramatic portrait of Osbaldistone Hall, Scott held firmly in mind the wider questions
of social change. They are: "For the division of labour in
every department not having then taken place so fully as
since that period."[2] Here Scott is using to keen satirical
effect the well-known fact that specialization increases as
the old agricultural and aristocratic organization breaks
down. The ample old days, he is saying in effect, when a
gentleman really was a gentleman, and lived on his own
land, and was respected by his tenants and servants were
also days when fine moral distinctions were impossible. Just
as a farm-labourer has to have a smattering of many skills, so
a gentleman might then have to be a bit of a rogue. The

---

[1] Chap 3.

[2] Such carefully considered historical passages give a particular air of futility to the extraordinary mistake in the date of the
action of this novel made by Georg Lukacs, who puts it 'several
decades' after *Waverley*, which deals with 1745. If several is
taken to mean about three, this represents an error of sixty years.
If it is generously taken to mean only two, it represents an error of
fifty years. M. Lukacs then proceeds to erect a complicated argument in economic history upon this gross error. M. Lukacs is one
of those men who pontificate on books they have not read, and
the tendency evident in some quarters to take his book seriously
can only be an obstacle to the understanding of Scott. (See *The
Historical Novel* by Georg Lukacs, trans. Hannah and Stanley
Mitchell. p58.)

strict commercial ethic, however narrow and selfish it is in essence, is bound to become more sympathetic.

But Frank's closer acquaintance with his uncle's family reveals a deeper malaise than this. Except perhaps to a romantic boy, disgusted with commercial standards, it is not surprising that the house of a Northumberland squire should be barbaric and bibulous. It is more than this. Frank and the reader sense only gradually that the tradition is being lost. Only the externals, the hunting and drinking, are being kept up. There is little enough family feeling or sense of tradition or care of dependants; and what there is, is almost all concentrated in the person of the father. The six sons represent a race that is spiritually dying. I do not defend the legerdemain by which Scott makes them disappear at the end, for it is a procedure more suited to an allegorical poem than to a novel, parts of which are realistic. But its meaning is clear enough. The sons disappear because their way of life is outmoded, and above all, because they have neither lived up to the ethos of this outmoded way, nor substituted a new one for it. Their Jacobitism is not really a principle or even a sentiment, but rather a hypocritical screen for the continued enjoyment of barbaric country customs.

Scott takes care that the tenderness associated with Diana Vernon does little to relieve this barbarous gloom. In the first place, she is herself a ruthless critic of the stupidity and debauchery of her relatives. But more telling than this is her way of defending the tradition. Urged by Frank to enquire into the Protestant arguments she says: "Hush! no more of that. Forsake the faith of my gallant fathers! I would as soon, were I a man, forsake their banner, when the tide of battle pressed hardest against it, and turn, like a hireling recreant, to join the victorious enemy."[1]

This passage forms a subtle, and perhaps a unique ex-

[1] Chap 9.

ception to what was said earlier about Diana's function. Its place in Scott's strategy is important. For it reinforces the identification, implicit in the whole book, between religious, spiritual and social traditions. Catholicism here has no autonomous life; it is no more than the distinguishing mark of a whole cluster of social attitudes and political opinions. This raises a point of general importance, to which I return at the end of this chapter. Furthermore, Diana's answer is charming but superficial. She does not challenge Frank's assumption that all the reason is on his side, and all the sentiment on hers. If this is the best that can be said for the Catholic and Jacobite cause by a charming and intelligent girl, whose sex excuses her from the reproach of merely feeling instead of thinking, how much stronger is the condemnation of men who have no such excuse, and whose sentiment for tradition is drowned in their graceless boorishness?

II

Scott had always an eye for hypocrisy. One might say that an interest in it was a function of a temperament like his, combining reckless flights of generous sentiment with the shrewdest assessment of everyday realities. He knew very well that in a time of civil war, canting self-interested camp-followers will always be found. And he was far too fair and sensible to suppose that they would all be on one side. In *Rob Roy* each side has its characteristic hypocrite, but even here the book's general anti-Jacobite tendency is apparent. Rashleigh is a hypocrite pure and simple. Because, as we have seen, his mental processes are not understood, he can have no excuse in the reader's eyes. Andrew Fairservice is quite a different matter. His religious hypocrisy is strongly rooted in that good old-fashioned peasant roguery, for which generous men of the world so often have a tender feeling.

Scott was never tired of reading and quoting Shakespeare's
Henry IV; and we are near the world of Justice Shallow
and Bardolph when Andrew says "This is no day to
speak o' carnal matters," casting his eyes upwards; "but
if it werena Sabbath at e'en, I wad speer what ye wad be
content to gie to ane that wad bear ye pleasant company on
the road, and tell ye the names of the gentlemen's and noble-
men's seats and castles and count their kin to ye?"[1] Besides
his position as the unwilling servant of a family alien to him
in religion, blood, and politics must provide some serious
excuse for the habit of hypocrisy.

Taking Andrew Fairservice and Frank's father together,
one might say that Scott has cleverly *disinfected* all the unpleasing features of the commercial Whig ethic. Money-
grubbing, cant, opinions formed by worldly interests—
every feature is there, but none is fatal to our respect. Scott
was a subtle advocate when he wished to be. If one compares
this with the blustering assertions and blatant omissions of
Carlyle and Froude[2] in supporting the same causes, one returns to Scott with an enhanced respect for what is perhaps
the quality most often forgotten or underrated in him, his
sheer intelligence. All the same, there is something lacking
here, which his greatest novels, especially *Waverley* and
Redgauntlet, abundantly possess. Here there is no serious
attempt to see as deep as possible into the motives and causes
of every relevant opinion. There were times when Scott,
like other very intelligent men, was tempted to be too
clever.

More direct and simple, however, and so more persuasive
in the end, is his treatment of Protestant worship and the
Scots Sunday. Here is Frank's account of the soothing effect

[1] Chap 18.
[2] This, of course, is *a fortiori*. Carlyle and Froude were very clever
men in their different ways.

of a Sunday evening in Glasgow on his distracted, impatient mind:

"Various groups of persons, all of whom, young and old, seemed impressed with a reverential feeling of the sanctity of the day, passed along the large open meadow which lies on the northern bank of the Clyde, and serves at once as a bleaching-field and a pleasure-walk for the inhabitants, or paced with slow steps the long bridge which communicates with the southern district of the county. All that I remember of them was the general, yet not unpleasing, intimation of a devotional character impressed on each little party, formally assumed perhaps by some, but sincerely characterising the greater number, which hushed the petulant gaiety of the young into a tone of more quiet, yet more interesting, interchange of sentiments, and suppressed the vehement argument and protracted disputes of those of more advanced age. Notwithstanding the numbers who passed me, no general sound of the human voice was heard; few turned again to take some minutes' voluntary exercise, to which the leisure of the evening, and the beauty of the surrounding scenery, seemed to invite them: all hurried to their homes and resting-places. To one accustomed to the mode of spending Sunday evenings abroad, even among the French Calvinists, there seemed something Judaical yet at the same time striking and affecting, in the mode of keeping the Sabbath holy."[1]

The British Sunday has, on the whole, had many to blame and few to praise it. This passage may be compared especially with the meditation of Dickens' Clennam ("Heaven forgive me, and those who have trained me. How I have hated this day.")[2] Scott's passage just quoted cannot rival the other in brilliance. But it is every bit as much a part of the book's organism. It not only contrasts with the Sunday at Osbaldi-

[1] Chap 21.　　[2] *Little Dorrit* chap 3.

stone Hall ("a day particularly hard to be got rid of"), it also shows that Fairservice's cant way of speaking about the Sabbath is a perversion of a good principle, not a memory of an evil one. Moreover, it prepares the way for the amusing but touching picture of Nicol Jarvie impatiently waiting till the clock strikes midnight before coming to the help of Frank and Rob Roy, reproaching himself at the same time for having thought more on worldly business that day than on the preaching. And Scott is not content with this account of the social blessings of Protestantism, but actually asserts, in Frank's person, the inherent superiority of Protestant over Catholic worship.

"I had heard the service of high mass in France, celebrated with all the *éclat* which the choicest music, the richest dresses, the most imposing ceremonies, could confer on it; yet it fell short in effect of the simplicity of the Presbyterian worship. The devotion, in which everyone took a share, seemed so superior to that which was recited by musicians, as a lesson which they had learned by rote, that it gave the Scottish worship all the advantage of reality over acting."[1] Scott must have known that he was putting a case here, and that a different case could be made. It is difficult to decide whether the one-sidedness springs out of the decision to tell the story in the first person, or whether the technique was found appropriate to the desired bias. But in either case the important point to notice is this. The partisan, first person view is the only one the book conveys. Scott never attempted and probably could not have wielded the arts by which Dickens in *Great Expectations* would make the first person account contribute to an objective picture of the narrator and all he stands for. Any answer to Frank must be sought in other books on the seventeenth and eighteenth century, not here.

[1] *Rob Roy* chap 20.

Nevertheless, Nicol Jarvie deserves a worthier opponent than the besotted squires of Northumberland; and if there is never any doubt who is to triumph, Rob Roy is worthy of his steel. He is a foil, but a good one. His real position in the book provides a caveat about the treatment of Scott's sources. Rob Roy, not Jarvie, was the myth to which the antiquarian and the spell-binder in Scott responded with enthusiasm. There were undoubtedly sides of his nature which found the brazen honour-seeking Highlander the more sympathetic of the two. In other books these romantic impulses were given a freer run; here they were sternly disciplined. Yet they could still provide a fruitful tension, and chapter 23, on the whole the most important in the book, forms a mixture of opposites that is extremely characteristic of the author. It is at the same time a complete vindication of Jarvie, and a foretaste of an ultimate reconciliation between all the conflicting loyalties that made men fight for and against the Jacobite rebels. One can see here the advantage Scott derived from the choice of 1715 here and of 1745 for *Waverley*. The aftermath of 1715 was not so bitter. The horror of the Highland clearances after 1745 was present to writer and reader, though not treated in the story, to intensify the pathos of the last chapters of *Waverley*. The less drastic consequences of 1715 permit a more hard-headed and a longer view.

Each man in his own way understands the honesty of the other. Rob Roy has broken into the Glasgow prison, and Jarvie as a magistrate and leading citizen has him entirely in his power, for, according to law, crimes enough can be proved against him.

" 'Ah, ye reiving villain!' interrupted Mr. Jarvie. 'But tell ower your sins, and prepare ye, for if I say the word'——

'True, Bailie,' said he who was thus addressed, folding his hands behind him with the utmost *nonchalance*, 'but ye will never say that word.'

'And why suld I not, sir?' exclaimed the magistrate—
'Why suld I not? Answer me that—why suld I not?'

'For three sufficient reasons, Bailie Jarvie.—First, for auld
langsyne;—second, for the sake of the auld wife ayont the
fire at Stuckavrallachan, that made some mixture of our
bluids, to my own proper shame be it spoken!' "[1]

The talk of shame here is only half jocular; but the solid
advantage to be derived from the shame is seized thank-
fully. Rob Roy has no difficulty in despising the class to
which Jarvie belongs and at the same time respecting his
different version of family loyalty, and his (from Rob Roy's
point of view) low, commercial type of honour. Jarvie, asked
if Rob Roy is honest, replies: " 'Umph!' with a precaution-
ary sort of cough,—'Ay, he has a kind o' Hieland honesty—
he's honest after a sort, as they say.' And illustrates the
qualification by quoting the example of a man who was
boasting of his loyalty to the King, and when asked how he
was serving the King when he fought in Cromwell's army at
Worcester, replied that he served him after a sort. But of the
highland honour he says: " 'Honour is a homicide and a
bloodspiller, that gangs about making frays in the street; but
Credit is a decent honest man, that sits at hame and makes
the pat play.' "[2] Scott has seen to it that Jarvie has shown
enough courage and generosity in his own way to be taken
seriously when he says this.

The sympathy which the reader feels for the hunted and
dispossessed Highlanders is filtered through Jarvie's generous mind. It is Jarvie that tells how " 'Rob cam hame, and
fand desolation, God pity us! where he left plenty; he looked
east, west, south, north, and saw neither hauld nor hope—
neither beild nor shelter; sae he e'en pu'd the bonnet ower
his brow, belted the broadsword to his side, took to the
brae-side and became a broken man.' "[3] This provides an

---

[1] *Rob Roy* chap 23.   [2] *Rob Roy* chap 26.   [3] Chap 26.

excuse for Rob, but our strongest impression is of Jarvie's extraordinary breadth of sympathy. It is he, too, only a page or two later who is allowed, a little surprisingly, to proclaim a feeling that we know from other sources to have been Scott's own. Comparing Rob Roy's exploits to those of Robin Hood and William Wallace, he says: " 'It's a queer thing o' me, gentlemen, that am a man o' peace mysell, and a peacefu' man's son, for the deacon my father quarrelled wi' nane o' the town-council—it's a queer thing, I say, but I think the Hieland blude o' me warms at thae daft tales, and whiles I like better to hear them than a word o' profit, Gude forgie me!—But they are vanities—sinfu' vanities—and, moreover, again the statute law—again the statute and gospel law.' "

How characteristic of the commercial ethic of the Protestant Lowlanders is that easy association between Gospel and statute; and how great are the ambiguities involved in that innocent word 'profit'. Scott is just as much aware of the ambiguities as Dickens was when he drew Mrs. Clennam. But he is making them point in the opposite direction. That is to say, that where Dickens and others make the religious profession appear as a hypocritical cloak for the pursuit of commercial profit, Scott turns the commercial talk into a cloak for generous impulses. Thus, Jarvie affects to take a strict commercial view, when he says: " 'He's a Hieland gentleman, nae doubt—better rank need nane to be;—and for habit, I judge he wears the Hieland habit amang the hills, though he has breeks on when he comes to Glasgow;—and as for his subsistence, what needs we care about his subsistence, sae lang as he asks naething frae us, ye ken.' "[1] This is hypocrisy in reverse, for he is concealing the £1000 debt owed to himself by Rob Roy which must appear to him at this stage unlikely to be paid. Here, we may feel, here we are certainly meant to feel, is the true version

[1] Chap 24.

of generous honour, purged of the waywardness and violence of the aristocratic tradition. We see how right Rob Roy was when he trusted absolutely to Jarvie's honourable silence in the prison. And then it is rather the wayward, violent Highlander, attractive though he is, who is the hypocrite, or, perhaps, if that is too strong a word, is guilty of intellectual dishonesty. To trust your life with perfect confidence to a man's delicate sense of honour takes away your right to sneer at his base commercial standards. Rob Roy knows this, but a few sneers at the vulgarity of the commercial ethic and the baseness of the Lowlanders are a sop required by his pride. An aristocrat cannot easily bear an obligation, and so, just when he is most deeply indebted to Jarvie for saving him he must say: " 'The devil damn your place and you baith! The only drap o' gentle bluid that's in your body was our great grand-uncle's that was justified at Dumbarton, and you set yourself up to say ye wad derogate frae your place to visit me!' "

And there is still another surprise in store. The reader is likely to think by now that he has taken the measure of Rob Roy's barbarity. It will have come to seem largely theoretical, a function of maladjustment to a new kind of society. But when he is introduced to Rob's wife he will see his error. Called an Amazon, compared to Jael, (the woman who pierced the head of the sleeping Sisera) and to Deborah, she is nearly an abstract idea of dignified female ferocity. She speaks with the kind of rhetoric which Scott slips into when he is sincerely moved by an idea, but has no more than a shadowy hold upon the personality of the speaker: " 'I could have bid you live, had life been to you the same weary and wasting burden that it is to me—that it is to every noble and generous mind. But you—wretch! you could creep through the world unaffected by its various disgraces, its ineffable miseries, its constantly accumulating mass of crime and sorrow; you could live and enjoy yourself, while the noble-minded are betrayed—while nameless and birthless villains tread on the neck of the brave and long-descended; you could enjoy yourself, like a butcher's dog in the shambles, battening on garbage, while the slaughter of the oldest and best went on around you! This enjoyment you shall not partake of; you shall die, base dog, and that before yon cloud has passed over the sun.' "[1]

It is hardly necessary to point out that this is poor stuff compared with Scott's best. But the importance of the cold-blooded killing, which immediately follows, in the story's strategy is considerable. It jerks us back from our comfortable contemplation of the domesticated barbarity of Rob Roy to an understanding of the true nature and consequences of this barbaric tradition. And the killing of Morris, shocking enough to us, may have been still more shocking to Scott's first readers. For two deeply-ingrained ideas which have partly lost their force were outraged—the feeling about military chivalry and the feeling about feminine modesty and tenderness. All this, of course, illustrates my original point about the book's nature. As a lawyer's argument it is brilliant; as a novel it is uneven, and, at times, perfunctory. Helen MacGregor's rhetoric may be poor, but the author's timing in placing her violent act is excellent.

And so it is that humbly and hesitantly Nicol Jarvie carries all before him with the reader even in the unfamiliar and daunting lair of Rob Roy himself. Jarvie is the hero, Jarvie is right, and Protestantism is right and the new commercial ethic, though admittedly capable of debasement, is right if held with honest and generous intentions. And the only counterweight is Rob Roy's eloquent lament in chapter 35 about the heather and his native hills. He is here saying something very like what Scott used to say *in propria persona*. But what might in another book have been near the

---

[1] Chap 31.

centre is here on the margin. A comparison with Baron Bradwardine's lament will come near to justifying the label anti-Waverley for the book as a whole.

To set a precise value on a book of this character is unusually difficult. Its brilliance as an argued case, and its shortcomings as a narrative have, I hope, been sufficiently indicated. Compared with Scott's very greatest achievements it has two grave limitations. It does not leave enough 'play'; it does not allow the 'wrong' cause enough autonomy, so that the reader either has to accept the argument through which he is led or else reject it. There is no moment of truth when the men and the causes can really speak for themselves, reveal to us their inner natures and leave the decision to us. The second point is perhaps ultimately a function of the first. The book is decidedly superficial in its treatment of the relation between religion and politics. It is sad to see the author of *Old Mortality* and *The Heart of Midlothian* treating religion almost as an epiphenomenon of class realities. But this 'Marxist' side of Scott's versatile intelligence was only one, and may be allowed its place.

4 *The Heart of Midlothian*

The generally obscure critical situation of Scott to-day is at its darkest and strangest in the case of *The Heart of Midlothian*. It has a kind of legendary repute as being his best book, an opinion supported by Dr. Leavis in the single paragraph he was able to spare for what he calls a 'great and very intelligent man' in *The Great Tradition*. Professor Davie devotes a short chapter to it (theoretically) in *The Heyday of Sir Walter Scott*, but this chapter turns out to be mostly about Pushkin, and partly about Wordsworth, and at the same time to contain a summary dismissal of the book's merits. The reasons given for the judgment are somewhat eccentric, for they consist mainly of complaints about the infelicity and prolixity of a few short passages of prose which are treated as being typical. I call this eccentric, not, of course, because I dispute the importance of brevity and precision, and not because I differ very much from Professor Davie about Scott's defects of style. I call it eccentric because I think that Scott's defects of style could be illustrated pretty well from any of his books—both the best and the worst. Moreover, if it is true, as most people would agree that it is, that many of Scott's finest passages are in the form of dialogue, it is a little unfair to concentrate entirely on defects in some, admittedly rather slack, narrative passages.

Now I think there are good reasons for a special critical confusion about this book over and above the generally confused critical situation regarding Scott's achievement as a whole. Some of these are obvious. The book is long, and unusually complicated in its intrigues, and unusually varied in scene and subject. It appears in its early chapters to be developing as a political study, but then veers to the most intimate psychological portrait (perhaps) in the whole of Scott's work. Moreover, certain scenes which the reader may have long foreseen and awaited are treated in a way that is not only surprising at the time but remains puzzling afterwards. Of these the most obvious, and perhaps most important, deviation from the expected is to be found in chapter 37, when Jeanie meets the Queen and pleads for her sister's life. The cumulative effect of all the surprises may be to make the whole impression left by the book ambiguous. And those who feel this ambiguity would probably maintain that it was different in kind from another commoner experience in reading Scott, which derives from his imaginative fairness. One may be in doubt at the end of *Waverley* about the relative value of the opposed civilizations; but one is in no doubt about the issues. If we are shown clearly the nature of the case, we can come to our own conclusions about values. The ambiguity of *The Heart of Midlothian* is deeper than that.

I do not know that this can be wholly explained; but part of the explanation seems to lie in Scott's own strange combination of contradictory attitudes on the question of crowd violence. The man who in a letter to his daughter-in-law of 21 April 1825 wrote a strong justification of the Peterloo 'massacre' was the same man who wrote less than four years later: "The mob have lost the spirit they had in Porteous' time or they would have taken the doctor under their own special ordering."[1]

That he should, like many other people, have had contrary emotions about Effie's unchastity is understandable

---

[1] *Letters* vol XI p94 dated 11 January 1829. The doctor was accused of buying the bodies of murdered men for anatomical research.

enough. But the significant point is that in no other book of his would a conflict of this kind be so important, for in no other are problems of sexual conduct at the centre.

It would seem that we have here a key example of the conflicts established in the work of an author who has so many different aims as Scott, and so often tries to achieve them all at once. Thus, if one set out to give an account of the book's moral organization, one could make it sound very neat. All the leading events turn on the relation between justice and mercy. First Wilson, the smuggler condemned to death, appeals to Porteous for the tiny mercy of the loosening of the handcuffs on the way to execution, and his request is refused. Then Porteous, having suppressed a riot against the execution with bloodshed, is first convicted, then pardoned by the Government, and then put to death by the crowd. But the crowd act theoretically, and to an extraordinary extent in practice, on the principle that they are carrying out a legal sentence which has been duly pronounced and then unjustly revoked by a corrupt government. In fact, the leaders of the crowd maintain that Porteous' treatment of Wilson was an example of a false show of justice and the denial of true mercy, while their own killing of Porteous is the performance of true justice, and the rejection of false mercy, or sparing the guilty through base favouritism.

The same issues are at stake in the story of Effie Deans. She is condemned by due order of law, and without manifest bias on the part of her judges. Nevertheless, the sentence involves a twofold injustice. There is an inherent injustice in the legal doctrine of constructive malice, which deduces a presumption of guilt from silence. There is an accidental injustice caused by false evidence and the mistaken interpretation of facts. But above all, the crucial point is that she is condemned by reason of her sister's inability to tell a lie.

One may well feel that here Scott presented the most

serious and the most difficult moral issue of his whole literary career. Those who admire the book above all his others are those for whom the importance of this issue, and the manifest dignity and power with which he presents it, not only outweigh all the book's defects, but even outweigh his success in some of his other books in creating more perfect works of art. Those who are unimpressed with this book, although admirers of Scott in general, are those who see him essentially as a historical novelist, that is an imaginative re-creator of the processes of cultural conflict and change. This party will be inclined to say that, however deep and serious the moral issue raised by Jeanie Deans' refusal to tell a lie, such an issue can only become the material of the highest art in the hands of an author possessing a subtler grasp of psychological processes than Scott could reach.

Neither of these views seems to me in itself entirely satisfactory. And, in order to judge more accurately we have to consider the links which Scott has tried to establish between the story of Porteous and Wilson, and the story of Effie and Jeanie. First, of course, the stories are linked in the person of Staunton or Robertson. Wilson's colleague in crime, who is condemned with him but escapes, is also the father of the child which Effie is wrongly convicted of killing. Here the book's opponents will point out that this link is superficial, and not much different from Scott's favourite disguise motif, which has to bear so much of the burden of construction in his more light-hearted works, such as *Ivanhoe*. They can also say with perfect truth that Staunton is a melodramatic figure, whose mental processes are given in a superficial way, and that such a character cannot have the real importance in the book that he is thus theoretically credited with. All this is true, but it should not be allowed to distract attention from the less obvious and more substantial links which Scott establishes.

Porteous and Effie are both enthusiasts. The procurator-

174

fiscal says of Porteous that "he never had ony fears, or scruples, or doubts, or conscience, about onything your honours bade him." To which the Bailie replies: "He was a gude servant o' the town, though he was an ower free-living man."[1] Loyal devotion, in the man's case to a discipline and duty, in the woman's case to love, and in each salted with passionate lack of control, leads in each case to a murder trial. In each case the evidence is confused and the legal decision arbitrary. The actions of Porteous have really resulted in deaths but his own degree of responsibility is dubious; Effie's actions never caused a death, yet all the evidence at the time points to one. But the similarity must not be pushed too far, for in one very important respect Porteous and Effie are opposites. Porteous has loyalty without generosity, and so he can bring himself to speak the words, which the Edinburgh crowd will never forgive. When Wilson, on his way to execution is suffering from the terrible pain of handcuffs that are too small for his wrists, Porteous says: "It signifies little, your pain will soon be at an end." Here the similarity is not between Porteous and Effie, but between Effie and Wilson. For it was Wilson, believing himself the more guilty of the two, who gave Staunton the chance to escape by clinging on to two of the guards, and calling to him to run. At points like this the link between the Porteous and Deans stories provided by Staunton can really tell, despite the latter's unconvincing psychological presentation. Wilson and Effie were not only loyal to the same man, but each made a heroic sacrifice for him, Wilson by holding on to the guards, Effie by refusing to name him as the father of her child.

So we have two contrasted criminals, Porteous and Wilson. The first is harsh, dutiful, and betrayed by zeal first into a cruel but legal act (the handcuffs), and then into violent and

[1] Chap 16.

illegal acts in support of law and order. Wilson is fundamentally lawless, but high-spirited and generous, and possessed
of that wonderful gift of seeing himself objectively in relation to other people. This leads him to distinguish between
his own crime and Staunton's and to decide that the major
responsibility is his own. It leads him also to reply to Porteous' cruel remark about the handcuffs (just quoted) "You
know not how soon you yourself may have occasion to ask
the mercy, which you are now refusing to a fellow-creature.
May God forgive you!" Now if Scott were Fielding we might
have to be content with this type of opposition; we might be
left with the comfortable feeling, so dear to law-abiding
citizens in relaxed mood, that their impartial generosity is
fully equal to perceiving the virtues of the criminal classes
and the petty limitations of the official mind. But the contrast Scott wishes us to have in mind is not a contrast of two
but of four. The third, of course, is Effie, who is like Wilson
in her imaginative capacity for sacrifice, but is not, like him,
deliberately lawless. She is here more like Porteous, as we
have seen, in carrying her proper feelings and loyalties to
the point where they become immoral, and are liable, if
circumstances are adverse, to become criminal as well.

The fourth term of the equation is the shadowy Staunton.
He is lawless, like Wilson, but ungenerous, like Porteous.
He is the beneficiary of the sacrifices of others; perhaps he
has some excuse for accepting Wilson's sacrifice, but he has
none at all for accepting Effie's. It is only if we keep the
implied contrast on the one hand with Wilson, and on the
other with Porteous firmly in mind that we shall understand
just what Scott was trying to do in the person of Staunton.
It was a magnificent conception not quite brought to fulfilment. When he first meets Butler he replies to questions
about himself with the words, "I am the devil."[1] When he

[1] Chap 11.

meets Jeanie and begs her to give the evidence needed to save Effie's life, he says, "I do *not* hope God will hear me at my need, I do not deserve—I do not expect that he will." And when Jeanie speaks of mercy to sinners he says: "Then should I have my own share therein, if you call it sinful to have been the destruction of the mother that bore me—of the friend that loved me—of the woman that trusted me—of the innocent child that was born to me."[1]

If we take these and all his other desperate sayings together, and bear in mind his actions, we shall see his theoretical position in the book's structure with perfect clearness. He is, or ought to be, a satirical portrait of the Byronic hero. He compensates for the meanness of his actions by the grandeur of his spiritual conception of guilt. He can blame himself inordinately but he must push the actual responsibility on to others. It is Jeanie, not himself, whom he expects to save the girl whose life he has, apparently, ruined. He compensates for his dread of ordinary responsibility in society by his reckless assumption of it in the world of spirit. The successor of the Giaour and Manfred, he is the ancestor of innumerable twentieth century anti-heroes.

In their original conception, then, these four characters were just the ones needed to hold together the structure of a book devoted to the search for true justice in the deceptive thickets of law and mercy. But there are several reasons why much of this scheme is shadowy and some of it remains a paper system. First and most obviously, Porteous and Wilson disappear from the scene too soon. This is not such a great drawback as it seems, for, without going into any minutiae of psychological analysis, Scott was able to give each one or two memorable phrases (quoted above) which sound through the whole book. Our sense of this is due, of course, not simply to their inherent eloquence and power but

[1] Chap 15.

to their exact relevance to what follows. Then to give full-length psychological portraits was not exactly Scott's métier. He did it remarkably well in the case of Jeanie, but his invention might have failed if he had attempted four in one book. However that may be, of one thing there can be no doubt. The Porteous passages, magnificent in themselves, are strategically out of place. If the birth of Effie's child had been advanced just a few months, so that the Porteous riots occurred between her trial and her reprieve, the resonance of the crucial exchanges between Porteous and Wilson would have been vastly increased. In attempting to make these exchanges tell from one end of the book to the other Scott was in the position of a very strong man attempting to lift a heavy weight at the full extent of his arm, instead of near the body.

But more fundamental than this point of technique is Scott's manifest unwillingness to give the mental processes of Staunton and Effie with the fullness of detail accorded to Jeanie and her father. No doubt he showed a sound comprehension of the limits of his own gift in not portraying their passionate love. But the remorse and fear which both feel so differently needs to be more than sketched. The result is that Jeanie herself holds in the book's structure something of the position of a tower without adequate foundations. In her person she reconciles the various conflicts of justice and mercy which the plot enacts and the other four characters in different facets represent. But the space accorded to her heroic journey to London, and the loving care lavished on her sacrifices are bound to seem out of proportion, when the characters who occasion them are not fully understood. Many a reader must have read the story as the simple celebration of the heroic Jeanie Deans. As such it is fine and good in its own way, but it lacks the full mastery and significance which it might have had. If it is read like this the author is as much to blame as the reader for the impoverishment.

The reasons for the comparative shadowiness of Effie's mental state are no doubt a little different from the failure to present Staunton in the round. Scott was able to present in memorable speech grand, simple feelings of a tragic character such as those afflicting Effie when accused of murdering the child she loved. And in chapter 25 he gives us a glimpse of his understanding of the jealous tensions built up in the mind of two sisters, one a virgin who could have saved her sister by a lie, the other whose love has brought her to the death sentence. But what his intelligence revealed to him, his bluff, man of the world delicacy partly rejected. Effie remains a sketch, but one in which every line is right, proving that only his natural reserve prevented him from giving the portrait in full.

The case of Staunton is more simple. Scott lacked some of the essential gifts of the satirist. Personally, the irresponsible Staunton requires satirical treatment; the exigencies of the plot, as well as Scott's general cast of mind seem to decree that he take part in heroic actions, which verge at times on the purely melodramatic. The satirical and melodramatic approaches can here only impede each other. And then it was difficult for a man of Scott's easy-going temper to blame severely anyone who suffered so much, even though he brought the suffering on himself, and wantonly imposed it on others. It is very much easier (for a novelist) to punish than to criticize. One might say, paradoxically, that Scott was too kind to Staunton in merely having him shot by his natural son. He should have remained alive and been made to *see*. Intellectually, Scott grasped the moral implications of the Byronic hero; temperamentally, he was unable to turn his understanding to full satirical account. The unmistakable sign of this kind of withdrawal in Scott's mind is to be found in Staunton's manner of speaking in the latter part of the book. The man who once spoke with terse desperation to Jeanie about saving Effie, now speaks to her like this: "While

I was engaged in desperate adventures, under so strange and dangerous a preceptor, I became acquainted with your unfortunate sister at some sports of the young people in the suburbs, which she frequented by stealth—and her ruin proved an interlude to the tragic scenes in which I was now deeply engaged. Yet this let me say—the villainy was not premeditated, and I was firmly resolved to do her all the justice which marriage could do, so soon as I should be able to extricate myself from my unhappy course of life, and embrace someone more suited to my birth."[1] This is not the voice of Staunton, but of Walter Scott, or rather one of his many voices, and that one of the least interesting. It is not the Augustan, not the original genius, not even the passionate antiquarian, but the kindly but prolix Edinburgh lawyer. It is only when Scott's imagination has temporarily failed, through haste or embarrassment or through a lack of clearness in the original conception, that he allows a character by nature so different from himself to speak with his own voice.

The above remarks have, I hope, not failed to suggest that Scott was attempting something grand, difficult and exceedingly relevant to our deepest dilemmas about the nature of justice and mercy. But they may also have given the impression that the attempt was a failure. This is not the impression I have intended to give, but the truth is that my account has not yet come to grips with the book's major strength. The gap between plan and achievement lies mainly in the points already noted, and especially in the relation the reader is meant to perceive between Jeanie, Effie, Staunton, Porteous and Wilson. But in its treatment of the practical working of justice and mercy in the world, the book is far more successful. Every major enactment of the conflict of justice and mercy really tells—the execution of Wilson, the pardoning followed by the killing of Porteous, Effie's trial,

[1] Chap 33.

Jeanie's mission, and Effie's reprieve. And these intelligently conceived and beautifully contrasted events are answered and enriched by the interior struggle of conscience between the irreconcilable principles of truth and affection in the minds of Jeanie Deans and her father.

I deal elsewhere[1] with the implacable logic of Scott's treatment of cause and effect, which is so finely present in the account of the Porteous riots. I am concerned here only with the bearing of these scenes on the whole picture of justice and mercy which the book presents. In a manner which by now should be familiar, Scott proceeds to defeat many of our usual expectations. The first assumption that has to be dropped is that justice comes from the head and mercy from the heart. Here is the crowd awaiting Porteous' execution: "Amid so numerous an assembly there was scarcely a word spoken save in whispers. The thirst of vengeance was in some degree allayed by its supposed certainty; and even the populace, with deeper feeling than they are wont to entertain, suppressed all clamorous exultation, and prepared to enjoy the scene of retaliation in triumph, silent and decent, though stern and relentless. It seemed as if the depth of their hatred to the unfortunate criminal scorned to display itself in anything resembling the more noisy current of their ordinary feelings."[2] When the reprieve arrives, there is at first a roar of indignation, and then: "The populace seemed to be ashamed of having expressed their disappointment in a vain clamour, and the sound changed, not into the silence which had preceded the arrival of these stunning news but into stifled mutterings . . . Yet still, though all expectation of the execution was over, the mob remained assembled, stationary, as it were, through very resentment, gazing on the preparations for death, which had now been made in vain, and stimulating their feelings, by recalling the various

[1] Chap 4, above.   [2] *The Heart of Midlothian* chap 4.

claims which Wilson might have had on royal mercy, from the mistaken notives on which he acted, as well as from the generosity he had displayed towards his accomplice." This mood of passionate reasonableness, not solely partisan, but attempting in its own way to be just, is a deeply significant point of comparison for all the other acts of justice and injustice, of mercy and indulgence which are to follow. The crowd here not only reveal to us the difficulty of distinguishing between justice and vengeance, but they reveal a more disturbing similarity between the feelings that excite people to vengeance and those that excite them to mercy. The strength of their pity for Wilson is the fuel of their hatred of Porteous. Moreover, the restraint so well described in the passage just quoted is maintained till the very end by those who take the lead in putting Porteous to death. In reply to Butler's question 'What hath constituted you his judges?', they reply " 'We are not his judges, he has been already judged and condemned by lawful authority' "[1] The suggestion is bound to occur, if they with their passionate devotion to vengeance can make such a good show of imitating the procedures of law, is the obverse also true? Is the serenity and formality of actual legal processes a mask of similar passions. This is just what we find when we come to Effie's trial.

When the jury find Effie guilty but recommend her to mercy because of "her extreme youth, and the cruel circumstances of her case" the judge replies: " 'I will undoubtedly transmit your recommendation to the throne. But it is my duty to tell all who now hear me, but especially to inform that unhappy young woman, in order that her mind may be settled accordingly, that I have not the least hope of a pardon being granted in the present case. You know the crime has been increasing in this land, and I know farther, that this

[1] Chap 7.

has been ascribed to the lenity in which the laws have been exercised . . .' "[1] This statement of the way in which law is administered only echoes the form of the law itself, where presumption of guilt takes the place of proof. The basis of both legal enactments and of the practical working of the law is the same; both are a matter of policy. This is more than miscarriage of justice. It is a general denial of justice both theoretical and practical.

All these ideas are certainly implicit in the story, but they are bound to seem a little abstract. Perhaps they seemed so to the author, for it was one of Scott's great strengths that he sincerely shared his readers' delight in the spectacular. The next few paragraphs are indeed spectacular, but their effect is much more than local, because of their exact representation of the deeper currents of thought. "When the Doomster showed himself, a tall haggard figure, arrayed in a fantastic garment of black and grey, passemented with silver lace, all fell back with a sort of instinctive horror, and made wide way for him to approach the foot of the table. As this office was held by the common executioner, men shouldered each other backward to avoid even the touch of his garment, and some were seen to brush their own clothes, which had accidentally become subject to such contamination. A sound went through the court, produced by each person drawing in their breath hard, as men do when they expect or witness what is frightful, and at the same time affecting. The caitiff villain yet seemed, amid his hardened brutality, to have some sense of his being the object of public detestation . . ."

In the silence which follows, Effie speaks:

" 'God forgive ye, my lords, and dinna be angry wi' me for wishing it—we a' need forgiveness.—As for myself I canna blame ye, for ye act up to your lights; and if I havena killed my poor infant, ye may witness a' that hae seen it this day,

[1] Chap 24.

that I hae been the means of killing my grey-headed father.
—I deserve the warst frae man, and frae God too,—but God
is mair mercifu' to us than we are to each other.' "[1]

This scene is worthy of careful study. The most difficult
things in Scott are sometimes those that look the easiest. Its
status as a grand, melodramatic moment is obvious. Its complexity can only be discerned in relation to the whole book's
argument. And Scott proceeds, as he so often does, by defeat-
ing expectation. He has placed Effie in a position where she
stands a clear, white, courageous figure in contrast to man
whose brutal presence is a walking emblem of the base calculations and unthinking violence which lie behind the ad-
ministration of law. He has prepared for this tableau by his
whole analysis of the lawless passions and law-abiding for-
malities of the slayers of Porteous. Then, when his grand
scene is ready, when his rhetorical phrases like 'caitiff villain'
are flowing freely, he turns back, a true balanced Augustan,
and allows Effie to remind us of her guilt. True, the words in
which she does so are themselves touching, and her conception of mutual forgiveness is sublime. But there is not
a trace in Scott of either of the two kinds of romantic falsification, which would at this point have afflicted so many
others. There is no 'inner purity of the fallen woman, hound-
ed down by unjust society'; there is no 'if only before that
day she could have fallen dead' as in so many of the novels
of the generation after that of Scott. There is just her sin,
her courage, her unjust conviction for a crime she did not
commit, and never could have contemplated. The excited
style, the startling opposition of black and white figures are
in a way deceptive, though certainly not insincere. They may
make us forget that a cool judge is watching, for whom two
wrongs never made a right, for whom the moral truisms in
the end are true, even though cruel and insensitive people

[1] Chap 24.
184

assert them uncharitably; and he is aware both that society is unjust, and that its controls are necessary for civilized life. Effie is magnificent here, but she is not his heroine. Jeanie is his heroine and her hard road to London must pay the price of Effie's fault.

It may now be easier to understand the significance of the comic treatment of some of the issues of justice and mercy. Take for instance Mrs. Saddletree's comment on the doctrine of constructive malice, according to which Effie can be presumed guilty of murder. " 'If the law maks murders,' she says, 'the law should be hanged for them; or if they wad hang a lawyer instead, the country wad find nae faut.' "[1] Clearly there is a sense in which the first part at least of this statement is unanswerably true. If we came upon it before we had got to know our author, we might either think that it heralded a *roman à thèse* attacking a concrete abuse of law, such as Wilkie Collins loved to write, or else that it introduced a tale glorifying the generous instincts above all laws and rules in the manner of Fielding. For Scott it is merely a point perceived by the shrewd peasant mind; the law is unjust, but it is in the nature of law to be unjust, and of mercy to be arbitrary. A truly just law is a phantom, and the absence of law would be the greatest injustice of all.

To complete our understanding of the book's whole statement about law and mercy we have to wait for Jeanie's interview with the Queen and Lady Suffolk. In scenes like this the master-storyteller and shrewd man of the world is so extraordinarily persuasive that it may be worth spending a moment considering what the reader is likely to expect of this long-prepared scene. First, he will be wondering what answer eventually awaits Effie's terrible cry of innocence before the law, coupled with moral guilt, which I have already quoted. Second, for many chapters between Effie's cry and

[1] Chap 5.

Jeanie's arrival in the royal presence, he has been concentrating on the heroism and hardships of Effie's sister. He may expect a touching scene in which the tears of the Scots lass melt the Queen's female heart, or a scene which shows pleas for justice unheard by cynical politicians. But he gets neither. Instead, he finds a strange political world, which might certainly be described as cynical. The Queen and the King's mistress are in league. The Queen has a 'masculine soul'; she is torn between her reluctance to grant anything to a convicted criminal who is a fellow-citizen of the Porteous rioters, and the political need to conciliate the Duke of Argyll, who could become such a powerful enemy to the established order, and such a valuable ally to the exiled Stuarts, if he cared to change his allegiance. The Queen looks on Jeanie with a connoisseur's eye and says: " 'She does not seem much qualified to alarm my friend the Duchess's jealousy.' " To this the Duke replies, " 'I think your Majesty will allow my taste may be a pledge for me on that score.' " *Taste*—not fidelity or honourable dealing.

Then Jeanie's directness of speech and ignorance of the affairs of the two women before her leads her to make two tactless remarks, which could be construed as references to the Queen's quarrel with her son, and to Lady Suffolk's position as a royal mistress. The impassioned plea comes at last, and the Queen is a little moved, but there can be no doubt that political motives prevail in the granting of the reprieve. If 'natural justice' is passionate, as in the killing of Porteous, and the operation of law is unjust, the prerogative of mercy here becomes a tainted political weapon. The Queen and the Duke do what Jeanie asks but they will never give her her due, and realize that she is a heroic human being. It is as if Effie's great appeal to the court had been granted in the letter and denied in the spirit.

But Effie's appeal had, implicitly, two parts. We have seen the ambiguous way in which her appeal for mercy from the law has been received. What about her plea for forgiveness from God and her father?

Scott shows his sense of the importance of this question by giving the internal struggles of Jeanie and her father the fullest treatment of all.

Here the date of the events in the book is particularly important. They come fifty or sixty years after the heroic days of the Lowland Whigs described in *Old Mortality*, and some twenty years after the first Jacobite rising of 1715. Davie Deans is an old man living on memories and traditions that are becoming every year more faint to his neighbours. In 1715 the interests and sentiments of the Lowland Whigs were on the same side as those of the Hanoverian government. This must have hastened the natural process by which the great and terrible days of Charles II and James II ceased to be vivid in the minds of the survivors, as those survivors became an ever smaller proportion of the population. It is clear that Deans feels this accidental coincidence of interest with the Government, begun in 1715, as a spiritual threat. It is clear also that his religion and temperament are best equipped to deal with times of crisis and suffering. In the quieter times that have succeeded since his youth, Davie Deans' religion has slightly ossified. It remains deeply sincere; and it is a sign of Scott's mastery of this whole subject that he can show the ossification so subtly and clearly without blurring or exaggeration. What has happened is that Deans, deprived of the natural food of a faith like his, persecution and scorn, has been driven back more and more on his own inner strength and self-righteousness. He is not, however much he wishes to be, quite a true seventeenth century fanatic. He does not rely directly on the voice of the Lord within his soul. The living water has ceased to flow, and only the rock is left. Scott uses the word 'Stoic' about his attitude to his daughter's disgrace and prospective execution.

" 'I have been constant and unchanged in my testimony,'

said David Deans, 'but then who has said it of me, that I have judged my neighbour over closely, because he hath more freedom in his walk than I have found in mine? I never was a separatist, nor for quarrelling with tender souls about mint, cummin, or the other lesser tithes. My daughter Jean may have a light in this subject that is hid frae my auld een—it is laid on her conscience, and not on mine—If she hath freedom to gang before this judicatory, and hold up her hand for this poor cast-away, surely I will not say she steppeth over her bounds; and if not'—He paused in his mental argument, while a pang of unutterable anguish convulsed his features, yet shaking it off, he firmly resumed the strain of his reasoning—'And IF NOT—God forbid that she should go into defection at bidding of mine! I wunna fret the tender conscience of one bairn—no, not to save the life of the other.'

A Roman would have devoted his daughter to death from different feelings and motives, but not upon a more heroic principle of duty."[1]

Now we shall be all astray if we do not feel and share Scott's deep respect for this tortured conscience, and any easy condemnations of 'Puritanism' are out of court. But two things will at once strike us as strange. The act he is contemplating is not (as Jeanie thinks through a misunderstanding) telling a lie to save Effie, for he mistakenly supposes that true evidence will be enough to save her. He is considering whether Jeanie would be right to go before a tribunal established by the state and give true evidence on oath. Now it is obvious from his words that he really thinks it right for her to do this. All his paternal instincts must reinforce this conviction. Yet he will not say a word to persuade her. The other point will emerge from taking this passage in the setting of the whole of Deans' character and conduct. When, we may ask, except here, has Deans ever

[1] Chap 18.

refrained from telling *anyone* what was the right thing to do, and least of all either of his daughters? Why does he not follow his dominating nature now, and advise Jeanie to give evidence, when the stakes are highest, the consequences so desperately important? The answer is suggested by the word 'Roman'. Scott is thinking here of aristocratic republican Rome, the world, for instance of Shakespeare's *Coriolanus*. A selfless devotion is being congealed into a personal pride. Deans (as his meditations about the choice in Jeanie's conscience show) has really abandoned, under the softening influence of time and the events of 1715, his belief in the inherent wickedness of submitting to the state in giving evidence. But his pride forbids him to advise his daughter; the most he can do is hope that she will make the decision herself.

Scott gives another subtle indication of his state of mind when he shows him deliberately avoiding in the daily reading of scripture any of the passages that would be applicable to the family's misfortune. A seventeenth century Covenanter would never have avoided such a natural source of aid and comfort. Who should believe more strongly in the relevance of the Bible to the everyday conduct of life than a believer in the Bible's verbal inspiration, and sole authority as a rule of faith? He did so because of that "stoical appearance of patient endurance of all the evil which earth could bring, which in his opinion was essential to the character of one who rated all earthly things at their just estimate of nothingness."[1] This is neither the spirit of the Gospel, nor of the early Covenanters. Indeed, his stoical pride is so strong that he can refuse to respond to the heart-breaking appeal of Jeanie: "O father, we are cruelly sted between God's laws and man's laws—What shall we do?—What can we do?"

The congealing effect of remaining in old traditions that

[1] Chap 14.

are no longer fully felt as activating the soul, leaves its slight traces even on the warm-hearted Jeanie. Thus she is tempted (though she soon rejects the temptation) to make a sophistical distinction between bearing false witness *against* our neighbour, and false witness *in favour* of a criminal. And when she goes to England her rigid education makes her write to her father in horror about 'the prelatists'; this horror is sincere, of course, but it is more a matter of early training than of personal conviction. Exclusiveness and security are not Jeanie's real style.

Now, of course, all this would be very trivial satire, if Deans or Jeanie were hypocrites, or did not really much care what became of Effie. But on a point of this kind Scott can be relied upon to go right. They do care intensely, the father with more sense of family honour, the daughter with more human tenderness. All the same, it is noticeable that the slight touch of unconscious hypocrisy which we have found in Deans' mind in the hour of crisis becomes more marked in the calmer times that follow. Thus, when Reuben Butler needs preferment in order to acquire funds to marry Jeanie, David Deans says: "However, ane gude hospitable gentleman, with whom it would be a part of wisdom to live on a gude understanding (for Hielandmen were hasty, ower hasty). As for the reverend person of whom he had spoken, he was candidate by favour of the Duke of Argyle (for David would not for the universe have called him presentee) for the kirk of the parish in which their farm was situated, and he was likely to be highly acceptable unto the Christian souls of the parish, who were hungering for spiritual manna. . . ."[1]

A little later Deans "altogether forgot to enquire whether Butler was called upon to subscribe the oaths to government." The slow but inexorable effect of political and cultural change working on an intensely stubborn, retentive

[1] Chap 42.

mind is complete. And nowhere in all his writings is Scott's sympathetic humanity more apparent. He 'Would not for the universe have *called* him presentee'. In its brevity, precision and cutting force the phrase is worthy of Swift. But the effect in the context is utterly unlike. Deans in his self-deception retains all his dignity, and much of our sympathy. And the wider implications, too, are different from any moral the great eighteenth century ironists from Swift to Hume would have found. For this gradual collapse of what they and Scott agree in calling 'fanaticism' is here only one part of the story. Instead of showing the decline (or advance) of fanaticism into Augustan realism, Scott shows a new version of the old faith in the person of Jeanie.

Just as Effie has two trials, one before the court in Scotland, and one in the backstairs of London court intrigue, so she has two spiritual trials, one in the mind of her father and one in the mind of her sister. And one notices, with some surprise, how little Jeanie says or thinks about her sister's sin, while so much of her energy is spent in her sister's cause. Jeanie too has her intractable moral problem; but it is unlike her father's, because it is faced without falsification and is exactly what it appears to be. Not, can she bend the knee to secular authority, but can she tell a lie? She cannot, but she can, by great sacrifice, repair the damage done to her sister by her refusal. So, in the person of Jeanie, the ossified covenanting tradition acquires a new spiritual life; and it is a genuine development, not a substitute. Jeanie is no deist, no Augustan observer of 'rational faith'. She is truly a child of her father in the spirit; she, without thought, by the sheer power of her truth and love, working on inherited tradition, guides the covenanting tradition back into a form which is viable in the new age, but more gentle and no less intense than the original form.

Scott's treatment of the great seventeenth century Protestant movement, and of its process of acclimatization into the unfriendly eighteenth century is more intelligent, more humane and more satisfying than that of so highly intelligent a man as Hume. The whole line of Scott's thought about history tends to check that reckless assumption of superiority over the benighted creatures of previous ages, which was so rarely questioned in the classical writings of the eighteenth century.

5 *Redgauntlet*

Design and accident alike mark *Redgauntlet* out as the last link in several different series. It appeared in 1824, Scott's last year of undisturbed, and, as it seemed, assured prosperity. It was his last serious attempt to reflect accurately upon his own early years. It was his last work of real distinction of any kind, and the last of three highly distinguished and beautifully contrasted meditations on the meaning of the Jacobite rebellions.

In *Waverley*, he had shown the meaning of the Jacobite struggle in terms of the clash of cultures and the general onward movement of history. In *Rob Roy*, without excluding a mild tribute to the romantic appeal of the old Highland tradition, he had shown the defeat of the Jacobites as part of a movement of cultural and economic progress seen as both inevitable and desirable. Both these books in their own way had covered the subject fully, but there was still a missing third term of which a man of Scott's cast of mind could not be oblivious. There was still the question of the meaning of defeat, of the power of memory and regret, of the spiritual value of adherence to a lost cause. In one sense, then, the theme here was much narrower than in *Waverley*, and Scott even deliberately emphasized its narrowness by setting the book in the 1760's, in the reign of George III, at a time when Jacobites were no longer felt by anybody as a serious threat. The schemes of Redgauntlet, the memories of Maxwell,

Pate-in-Peril, the dreams of romantic old ladies could easily be dismissed as shallow eccentricities.

Scott sees that as clearly as the reader does, and in a certain sense, he accepts such a contemptuous dismissal as just. But he sees too that in another way *Redgauntlet* has a deeper subject than *Waverley*, and a more general one— deeper because it deals with loyalty at a psychological rather than at a social level, and more general because the book's discoveries and conclusions are applicable to the support of the lost cause as such, instead of depending, as *Waverley* does, on the actual state of eighteenth century Scots society.

Many readers, I think, have been a little disconcerted by the book's unusual structure, and some have been bored by the earlier part, the exchange of letters between Alan Fairford and Darsie Latimer. We may be inclined to feel that in the first third of the book Scott was trying to be Richardson, and that a third of the way through he fortunately realized that he never would be. The switch to narrative is indeed clumsy enough, beginning with a tiresome paragraph of excuse and justification. All the same, something of value is achieved by those letters, and the curious *doubling* of the familiar figure of the experiencing young man, Waverley or Morton, or Francis Osbaldistone, is full of significance.

In the first place, autobiographical elements are stronger here than elsewhere. Scott was in truth a many-sided man, but perhaps in any case it is true that no one ever sees himself as a simple personality. The contrast between the two young men in the novel springs out of a contrast in the author's own nature which by now he was able to analyse with detachment. The clear-headed and formidably determined young lawyer and the lazy dreamer are aspects of himself that he understood. As a technical narrative device also the double hero is important. For Scott's usual method of making the hero 'the man between', torn by opposing forces, and oscillating in his own loyalty, could not have been effective here. The reasons why it could not be used again will reveal something about the book's inner nature and its unlikeness to what had gone before. Here neither Fairford nor Latimer is really in doubt as to which side he supports. Darsie Latimer's involvement with the Jacobite cause is hereditary and imposed upon him by force more than by persuasion. Scott even resisted the obvious temptation to make the romantic Green Mantle who had actually put down the gage of challenge at George III's coronation feast into a dyed-in-the-wool Jacobite. She, like Darsie, sees her uncle's 'errors'. Darsie Latimer, though a young man of spirit and courage, becomes through circumstances little more than his uncle's instrument for most of the book's course. When we understand this we see that a 'man between' of the Waverley type is not appropriate here. The Jacobite cause is now too remote to appeal to the young. There are only two ways left of adhering to it, by being fanatical like Redgauntlet himself, or by being nostalgically unwilling to abandon old memories like Maxwell and others in the book. The book is, above all, a study of memory and nostalgia; and so the function of the young is to show the face of the new world that does not remember, and finds it hard to admit that others do remember, and that some of them also deeply care.

The young men help Scott, too, with the very delicate task of putting Redgauntlet in perspective. A man of his character and history in a novel naturally tends to become either a monster or a superman; but he is neither, and Scott was determined here (one cannot say this of all his books or all his heroes) to get it right. He proceeds then in the opening epistolary section by some sighting shots, or what the gunners call bracketing. Here is Darsie Latimer's impression of Redgauntlet: "An air of sadness, or severity, or of both, seemed to indicate a melancholy, and, at the same time, a haughty, temper. I could not help running mentally over the ancient heroes to whom I might assimilate the noble form and countenance before me. He was too young, and evinced too little resignation to his fate, to resemble Belisarius. Coriolanus standing by the hearth of Tullus Aufidius came nearer the mark; yet the gloomy and haughty look of the stranger had, perhaps, still more of Marius seated among the ruins of Carthage."[1]

And here is Allan Fairford's view as he sees him on a visit to the house of Fairford senior: "I can only say, I thought him eminently disagreeable and ill-bred. No, 'ill-bred' is not the proper word; on the contrary, he appeared to know the rules of good-breeding perfectly, and only to think that the rank of the company did not require that he should attend to them—a view of the matter infinitely more offensive than if his behaviour had been that of uneducated and proper rudeness. While my father said grace, the laird did all but whistle aloud . . ."[2] The first passage is touching in its youthful enthusiasm, but faintly absurd. It is precisely this shallow romantic attitude to the end of the Jacobite tradition that Scott needs to exorcize. He does so in the neatest way by giving this attitude its head in the early pages through Darsie Latimer's letters, and then showing by what follows how superficial it is. One might say that most of the merchants of romantic Jacobitism in fiction who later supposed themselves to be followers of Walter Scott were really no more than followers of Darsie Latimer.

Alan Fairford's account is not so easy to assess. In a sense it is unexceptionable, and it is in fact very near to the usual tone in letters and conversation upon political subjects of Sir Walter Scott, Bart., of Abbotsford. But when his artistic powers are really awakened, Scott knows that, though judgments like this do not cease to be accurate, they cease to be adequate. Just how much they forget of what springs from

---

[1] *Letter* 4.   [2] *Letter* 5.

the deepest sources of personality the rest of the book will show.

I have said that *Redgauntlet* is, before everything else, a study of memory. It is important to remember that it is a multiple, balanced study not an intensive personal study. Redgauntlet as the central figure would never emerge, as he does, as a tragic hero without a complicated system of comparisons and contrasts. Scott shows us a society confronted with one of life's recurrent problems, how to remember and how to forget. Here is a political cause to which some have devoted their life, while others have devoted a good part of their energies to its defeat. Twenty years before this movement has seriously threatened to overturn a whole new order of society. Now it is irrevocably defeated. How is each man, and each class of man, enthusiast and Laodicean, landowner, lawyer, smuggler and merchant to cope with these memories? How can one disengage from such intense experience?

It is a kind of corporate, political equivalent of mourning a dead wife or friend, but with the important difference that causes do not die on one particular day, and death certificates cannot be issued. Appropriately, to show this process at work, Scott has given us an unusually wide, almost Dickensian, range of social types. The elder Fairford, Foxley, Maxwell, Wandering Willie, Nanty Ewart and others—all fulfil two functions at once. They broaden the view presented of the general public process of remembering and forgetting and they show by contrast the uniqueness of Redgauntlet's character and the loneliness of his position.

Fairford senior sets the general tone of Edinburgh society, the background against which this interior drama is differently lived by each person more deeply concerned. "He spoke sometimes of the Chevalier, but never either of the Prince, which would have been sacrificing his own principles, or of the Pretender, which would have been offensive to those of others. Again he usually designated the rebellion as the 'affair' of 1745, and spoke of anyone engaged in it as a person who had been 'out' at a certain period."[1] Of course, Scott sees with his usual good-natured shrewdness that it is impossible to distinguish here between the genuine courtesy of a man who respects all sincere opinions, and the well-developed commercial sense of the practising lawyer. Such a man does not react even to the direct provocation, which he receives from Redgauntlet, but only reflects that if he were Pope and Pretender both he would still have to find a good dinner for a man who had proposed himself as a guest.

But there are very different kinds of lukewarmness, just as there are of enthusiasm. A good contrasting case is Matthew Foxley, the Cumberland magistrate before whom Redgauntlet and Darsie Latimer his nephew appear. Here the *quieta non movenda* principle has a different basis. Mr. Foxley is a coward and wishes to be on the right side of Government. For him to know who Redgauntlet is, to know that his neighbour Herries of Birrenswork is the same man, is an entirely different thing from being officially seen to know it.

" 'Neighbour', he said, 'I could not have thought this; or I—eh—*did* think—in a corner of my own mind as it were —that you, I say—that you might have unluckily engaged in —eh—the matter of the Forty-Five—there was still time to have forgot all that.'

'And is it so singular that a man should have been out in the Forty-five?' said Herries with contemptuous composure. 'Your father, I think, Mr. Foxley, was out with Derwentwater in the Fifteen.'

'And lost half of his estate,' answered Foxley, with more rapidity than usual; 'and was very near—hem—being hanged into the boot. But this is—another—guess job—for— eh—fifteen is not forty-five; and my father had a remission,

[1] Narrative chap 1.

and you, I take it, have none.' And after a few more exchanges, Foxley reveals the essence of his thinking on the matter: 'While you were a good companion in the field, and over a bottle now and then—I did not—eh—think it necessary to ask into your private affairs. And if I thought you were—ahem—somewhat unfortunate in former undertakings, and enterprises, and connexions, which might cause you to live unsettledly and more private, I could have—eh —very little pleasure—to aggravate your case by interfering, or requiring explanations, which are often more easily asked than given. But when there are warrants and witnesses to names—and those names, Christian and surname, belong to —eh—an attainted person—charged—I trust falsely—with —ahem—taking advantage of modern broils and heartburnings to renew our civil disturbances, the case is altered; and I must—ahem—do my duty.' "[1]

But in between these two passages, Redgauntlet (Herries) has actually seized the warrant and burnt it with his own hand before he could be prevented. Instead of treating this lawless act of defiance as an aggravation, the justice and the clerk are pleased to discover that they cannot act on a warrant that no longer physically exists, and the whole ends with Foxley and Redgauntlet sharing a drink ordered for the justice and everyone else present by the destroyer of the warrant.

It is worth noting that Foxley is seen by Scott in a slightly unexpected way. *A priori*, one might think there were only two ways of treating such a man, either with broad humour or with indignant satire. But the intensely social cast of Scott's mind leads him to do something else, though he does not neglect to make the scene amusing. The Foxleys however inglorious, are seen as necessary. Through them the wheels are oiled, through them the damage done to society

[1] Narrative chap 7.

by the deep divisions of the past will be cured a little more easily and a little sooner.

Crosbie, the Provost who introduces young Fairford to Maxwell, 'Pate-in-Peril' is slightly different again. He sounds almost like Fairford senior when he says: "One may love the kirk, and yet not ride on the rigging of it; and one may love the king, and yet not be cramming him eternally down the throat of the unhappy folk that may chance to love another king better. I have friends and connexions among them, Mr. Fairford, as your father may have clients; they are flesh and blood like ourselves, these poor Jacobite bodies—sons of Adam and Eve, after all . . ."[1] but we soon see that these humane words have not the same genuine source as the courtesy of Fairford senior. Crosbie is ingeniously explaining away his own timidity, so that Maxwell's judgment is found in the end to be just: "The last word has him, speak it who will; and yet, because he is a whilly-wha body, and has a plausible tongue of his own, and is well enough connected, and especially because nobody could ever find out whether he is a Whig or Tory, this is the third time they have made him provost!"

All these characters that I have discussed so far are moderates, of course. Before turning to the Jacobites, we feel inclined to ask, 'What has happened to the fanatics on the other side, where are the Covenanters, heirs to the tradition of *Old Mortality*?' The answer, so far as this book goes, is a sad one. They have declined into cant and hypocrisy. A coarsened and insincere version of their religious rhetoric is found in the mouth of the smuggler Trumbull, who puts Fairford in touch with Nanty Ewart and the *Jumping Jenny*, and who cares, as Nanty truly says, for nothing of the trade but the profit. Now, of course, the insincere profession of a doctrine by a crook in no way invalidates its truth or value.

[1] Narrative chap 12.

But I think that Scott meant something rather more by Trumbull's covenanting rhetoric than just a criminal's cloak of respectability.

Here is an example of Trumbull's style on the occasion when Fairford goes to him with Maxwell's letter addressed to Redgauntlet:

" 'Do you know Mr. Maxwell of Summertrees?' said Fairford. 'I have heard of such a gentleman in the country-side, but have no acquaintance with him,' answered Mr. Trumbull. 'He is, as I have heard, a Papist; for the whore that sitteth on the seven hills ceaseth not yet to pour forth the cup of her abomination on these parts.'

'Yet he directed me hither, my good friend,' said Alan. 'Is there another of your name in this town of Annan?'

'None,' replied Mr. Trumbull, 'since my worthy father was removed; he was indeed a shining light. I wish you good-even, sir.'

'Stay one single instant,' said Fairford; 'this is a matter of life and death.'

'Not more than casting the burden of our sins where they should be laid.' "[1]

Trumbull is clearly an extreme case, and an unfair one to take to represent the Lowland Whigs. But Scott had done full justice to the Lowland Whigs in other books. The point here is rather the effect of historical circumstances upon the principles and temperament of fanatics. To retain our respect and his self-respect a fanatic has to be on the losing side. Redgauntlet whose plans will never even approach success is the fortunate one. And so Trumbull is relevant here in a way that a more respectable and moderate development of the seventeenth century Covenanter in the next century, (like Bailie Nicol Jarvie in *Rob Roy*) would not have been.

---

[1] Narrative chap 12.

II

Apart from Redgauntlet himself the character that contributes most to the study of Jacobite memories is Maxwell 'Pate-in-Peril', and when we consider how apt Scott is, like every writer who composes rapidly and with ease, to be prolix and repetitive, the economy of the presentation is striking. The important eleventh chapter establishes him as a necessary link in two senses. In the working of the story he is the man who can introduce Fairford to his old friend Redgauntlet, so that he can challenge him about Darsie Latimer's safety. His position in the map of feelings and attitudes corresponds exactly to this. He allows us to see the power of the ancient flame in an elderly, prudent, comfort-loving man so that we can in the end come to accept the reality of the total commitment of the dedicated servant of the cause, Redgauntlet. First he tells the old story, which we guess he has so often told before at Crosbie's dinner-table, of his capture after the Forty-Five; " 'Ye have heard of a year they call the Forty-Five, young gentleman; when the Southrons' heads made their last acquaintance with Scottish claymores? There was a set of rampauging chields in the country then that they called rebels—I never could find out what for. Someone should have been wi' them that never came, provost —Skye and the Bush aboon Traquair for that, ye ken. Weel, the job was settled at last. Cloured crowns were plenty, and raxed necks came into fashion. *I dinna mind very weel what I was doing, swaggering about the country with dirk and pistol at my belt for five or six months or thereaway; but I had a weary waking out of a wild dream!*' "[1]

[1] My italics. And some people are fond of telling us that Stendhal and Tolstoy were the first novelists to perceive the disorder and aimlessness of war as experienced by the soldier!

He goes on to tell how he was captured, handcuffed to Redgauntlet's elder brother, and, as we are to learn, the dead father of Darsie Latimer, and how he escaped, but his companion was executed.

At this stage Maxwell's narrative, though direct and moving in its language, has something in it of the ritual performance. The speaker is telling the truth and has been a brave fighter, but he is also a comfortable man of advancing years with a stake in the country, respected by his neighbours and ignored by the Government. The skill of the narrative that follows lies in a gradual alteration of the perspective so that a Jacobite rebellion, which here seems comfortably distant, becomes an immediate issue, and this in turn prepares for the final tableau in which we see that our first view was right and it is immeasurably distant after all.

When Maxwell has finished his time-honoured narrative, Crosbie says, as Maxwell 'looked round with an air of triumph for sympathy and applause,' "Here is to your good health; and may you never put your neck in such a venture again."

'Humph! I do not know,' answered Summertrees [Maxwell]. 'I am not like to be tempted with another opportunity. Yet who knows?' And then he made a deep pause."

But a few moments later he is saying: 'We may have our day next.' How exactly Scott catches the wavering tone, the feeling changing from moment to moment for reasons both serious and trivial—trivial because when he speaks of 'our day', he has of course had a glass or two more wine, serious because he has suddenly felt again with its original force the old sorrow of his friend's execution, which in his eyes was murder in cold blood.

Then Maxwell speaks of the surviving brother, the Redgauntlet of the novel, and says: " 'As all his own property was seized upon and plundered, he would have wanted common necessaries, but for the attachment of a fellow who

was a famous fiddler—a blind man. I have seen him with
Sir Henry myself, both before the affair broke out and while
it was going on. I have heard that he fiddled in the streets
of Carlisle, and carried what money he got to his master
while he was confined in the castle.'

'I do not believe a word of it,' said Mrs. Crosbie, kindling
with indignation. 'A Redgauntlet would have died twenty
times before he had touched a fiddler's wages.'

'Hout fie—hout fie, all nonsense and pride,' said the laird
of Summertrees. 'Scornful dogs will eat dirty puddings,
cousin Crosbie; ye little ken what some of your friends
were obliged to do yon time for a soup of brose or a bit of
bannock."

This passage is particularly important, and not just because it makes a new link for the reader who is sure to guess
that the fiddler is the same as the teller of the tale of the
recovery of the receipt from hell. It is more subtly important
in bringing the Forty-Five back from the limbo of lachrymose
after-dinner memories into sharp, immediate focus. The last
words of Maxwell quoted are war as it really is, and we notice
that in that formal and courteous society Maxwell is sufficiently stirred with the humdrum, low truth of his memories
to contradict a lady sharply. The chapter as a whole without
sacrificing the psychological truth of Maxwell's own response, brings the distant memories nearer, restores their
vividness, so that the unobtrusive effect upon the reader is
nearly that of moving backwards in time. We are being prepared for the strange re-enactment of the ancient drama by
Father Bonaventure and Redgauntlet. But this idea of the
stirring into renewed life of memories dulled by familiarity,
has already been announced in the strangest and most celebrated passage in the whole book, Wandering Willie's Tale,
of which Maxwell has just been allowed to remind us. There
are many aspects of this story, considered simply as a story,
that cannot be treated here. The point here is a rather

neglected one, its relevance to *Redgauntlet*. It is fairly clear from several indications that Wandering Wilie's Tale is not a tale of the supernatural, but of the hypnotic power of memory. Steenie, the hero of Willie's tale, under the influence of despair and brandy, perceives a visionary re-enactment of the wickedness of the old days: "There was the Bluidy Advocate Mackenzie who for his worldly wit and wisdom, had been to the rest as a god. And there was Claverhouse, as beautiful as when he lived, with his long, dark, curled locks, streaming down his laced buff-coat, and his left hand always on his right spule-blade, to hide the wound that the silver bullet had made." Now Claverhouse, who had been such a powerful figure in *Old Mortality*, died in 1689, so the intense folk-memory has lasted for three-quarters of a century. That it is confused memory and not just dream is shown by a passage that follows shortly: " 'Then ye maun eat and drink, Steenie,' said the figure; 'for we do little else here; and it's ill speaking between a fou man and a fasting.' Now these were the very words that the bloody Earl of Douglas said to keep the king's messenger in hand, while he cut the head of MacLellan of Bombie, at the Threave Castle, and that put Steenie mair and mair on his guard."[1] (In a characteristic note, Scott refers us to Pitscottie's *History of Scotland*, thus indicating that what Steenie remembered was truly historical.)

Enough has been said, I hope, but a detailed study of the story will show more clearly, to indicate how misguided is the common tendency to separate off Wandering Willie's Tale as a brilliant short story that just happens to come in *Redgauntlet*. Scott wrote many historical novels, but in all the others the aim is to get back to contemporary feelings, to experience the past as it was to those who lived in it, as a present reality. In *Redgauntlet*, the point is the opposite, to

---

[1] *Letter* 11.

show the power in a comparatively recent past period of memories of a more distant past. Only in this setting, then, could Wandering Willie's Tale reverberate through the book as it does here. The folk memory is as tenacious as the gentlemanly, and considerably more terse in expression. Speaking of the same dead Redgauntlet to whom Maxwell was handcuffed, and the man to whom he had given unbounded loyalty, Wandering Willie only says; " 'Mony a merry year was I wi' him; but wae's ma! he gaed out with other pretty men in the Forty-Five—I'll say nae mair about it!' "

Maxwell and Wandering Willie help to do for the reader what Redgauntlet tries so hard to do for his nephew, to prepare him for the appearance of the Pretender. Scott, we know, was over-fond of disguised kings and princes. This is one of the few cases where the disguise really tells. It is natural enough, of course, in itself that he should be disguised at this juncture. But much more important, if he were not disguised, Darsie Latimer could have no chance to see him as he is. The word 'Pretender' has too strong a resonance; everyone must have had an engrained idea about him, so that an unprejudiced view would have been impossible for anyone who met him *in propria persona*. But in a deeper sense, too, the disguise is appropriate. For, as he speaks to Latimer in chapter 16, we gradually feel the presence of a man of remarkable force of will half-unwillingly playing a part. He is in his forties, but 'care or fatigue, or indulgence had brought on the appearance of premature old age'. The glancing, uncertain references to his object in returning to Britain all show lack of confidence. " 'The cloud must soon rise,' he says, 'or it must sink upon us for ever!' " The melancholy dignity of the exchanges between the Pretender and Latimer is shattered suddenly by the entrance of the mistress, whose presence the Prince is anxious to hide from his followers. Immediately, the Prince's spell is broken, and it is not at first easy to see why. Admittedly, the Prince's priestly disguise makes her appearance particularly inappropriate. But we do not yet know anything of the special reasons the Prince's loyal followers have for distrusting her. Why, we may wonder, should a mistress make any difference to political prospects? There had been plenty of mistresses at the courts of the Prince's ancestors as at those of some of their Hanoverian opponents.

In fact, the entrance of the Prince's mistress changes the atmosphere fundamentally. The interview is taking place in the house of two devout spinsters, whose Jacobitism is only a consequence of their Catholic devotion. Now we are reminded that the real political contest has to be fought in the ordinary, workaday world, where religion is a weaker motive than selfishness, where pride, lust and obstinacy are stronger than principle. Moreover, the girl shatters the Prince's air of unquestioned command. She is not afraid of him, she can be rude to him, and he is perhaps even a little bit afraid of her. All this is effective at the moment, and also an admirable preparation for the final break between the Prince and all but one of his last supporters.

The effect is not just the crude 'idol with feet of clay'. The Prince remains a brave soldier, and, as he understands the term, an honourable gentleman. But he becomes a man aiming at political power, whose success will be determined by the forces he can command. The remote spiritual aura with which his unworldly hostesses and, in a more robust way, Redgauntlet himself have contrived to invest him is dispelled. Events must take their course.

It is notable, in this connection, that both the Prince and Redgauntlet, but especially the latter, speak fatalistically. Redgauntlet even denies the freedom of the will. At first sight they may seem to be in perfect harmony with what the whole book is saying. But there is a difference between their fatalism and Scott's, and that difference is crucial. Scott's is a kind of rational fatalism. His idea of the inevitable is the resultant of all the prevailing causes, including free human choices. Redgauntlet and the Prince cling desperately to a more primitive view of fate, which assumes that *anything* may be fated to happen. This has, for them, the great advantage that the apparently improbable event (such as a Jacobite Restoration) is really just as probable as one universally expected. Scott shows us great events being determined by sufficient causes and not by accidents.

At last in chapter 22 comes the meeting for which the whole book has been a preparation. We soon find that Redgauntlet is the only true fanatic left among the remnants of the old Jacobite families. Maxwell is there, but when he says, 'I have little to lose; they that took my land the last time may take my life this', the English gentleman still in possession of their estates look doubtful. The last representative of Anglican legitimism from Oxford is disturbed about the Prince's hereditary Catholicism. Some of them take to quarrelling among themselves, and there is even talk of duels, as if the frustrated bond of honour that binds them to memories of the House of Stuart has to find an outlet in 'honourable' squabbling about trifles. They insist that they have only come to attend a consultation, not a council of war, and they feel more dismay than joy at the surprising news that the Prince is actually present in the house where they are meeting. Unwilling to commit themselves to action and equally unwilling to admit that they will do nothing, they turn almost eagerly to the one specific cause of complaint they can find. The Prince has neglected the condition of dismissing the mistress who appeared earlier during the conversation between the Prince and Latimer, and who is suspected of being a spy of the Hanoverian court.

A small deputation then attend the Prince to press this essential condition. The inner disharmony of the whole gathering is revealed at this moment. As the Prince makes an

208

appropriate, but somewhat rhetorical speech, to the men who he thinks are joyfully welcoming their sovereign, the others stand in embarrassment, waiting to press the disagreeable matter of the mistress's dismissal. But Redgauntlet's anxiety is more acute than theirs, as the Prince pretends not to have heard of the condition that Redgauntlet had laid before him in writing before he began his voyage to England. He fears for his own honour and reputation. He promised to lay this condition before the Prince, and he afterwards swore that he had done so. If the Prince denies it, who will believe him? But the Prince is not really telling a lie. He soon makes it clear that he did receive notice of the condition. His denial is a proud refusal to take notice of a personal affront, which is also in his eyes an act of disloyalty to himself as sovereign. His denial of knowledge of the condition is a gracious Act of Oblivion solemnly proclaimed by a Prince without subjects. " 'In affairs of state and public policy,' he says, 'I will ever be guided, as becomes a prince, by the advice of my wisest counsellors; in those which regard my private affections and my domestic arrangements I claim the same freedom of will which I allow to all my subjects.' " And he goes on to declare with obstinate dignity that he is speaking not of a point of passion but of principle. He could part with the lady without a moment's regret but, 'if the axe and scaffold were ready before the windows of Whitehall, I would rather tread the same path with my great-grandfather than concede the slightest point in which my honour is concerned.' " Then, becoming really angry, he taunts his doubting and dissatisfied adherents with the thought that they might make their peace with Government by betraying him. At this point Sir Richard Glendale, driven beyond his patience pronounces what is in effect the last epitaph upon the Stuart cause: " 'My God, sire! of what great and inexpiable crime can your Majesty's ancestors have been guilty, that they have been punished

by the infliction of judicial blindness in their whole generation.' "

Both men are speaking here, of course, hastily and un-
guardedly. Yet what rises to the surface is in a way the very
essence of the Jacobite question. The Prince, not his followers (except Redgauntlet) is here the true Jacobite. The
Jacobite cause can make no sense unless loyalty to the true
hereditary king is an unconditional duty. What the Prince's
angry, unfair words really do (they are unfair because none
of those present is capable of betraying the Prince to the
Government) is to prove to Sir Richard that he was not really
in the end a Jacobite at all. Not that he was insincere, but
that he had not until this moment truly understood himself.
The Prince presents him with the pure milk of the word, and
he finds that in spite of years of sentimental loyalty, and
some sacrifice and risk, he has never been a true believer.
This effect of suddenly discovering what has really been true
all along is achieved by a perfectly natural quarrel.

But are the half-hearted adherents really changed in their
purpose by the Prince's neglect of their condition of dismissing the mistress, or do they seize on this as the most
plausible excuse for doing nothing? It is characteristic of
Scott when, as here, his psychological grasp is most sure that
he does not answer that question. The men themselves do not
know; both explanations are in a way satisfactory. Scott in
his greatest moments always stands for the ultimately un-
fathomable autonomy of the human spirit. One can see what
people do, one can record what they think, but there are
cases where the ultimate balance of motives is beyond us. It
is this more than anything else perhaps that marks him off
from the other great tradition of which Jane Austen was the
finest representative in his time.

But now with Redgauntlet and the Prince revealed as the
only true Jacobites remaining, all thought of military action

is abandoned. The question is how to cover the Prince's retreat, and he angrily says that he will shift for himself and trust to the Highland robbers and cattle-drovers, as he had done in the Forty-Five.

But it is too late; their meeting has been betrayed by Cristal Nixon, and no sooner does Redgauntlet receive a message warning him of the approach of Government troops, than in the general confusion that follows; "A gentleman, plainly dressed in a riding-habit, with a black cockade in his hat, but without any arms except a *couteau-de-chasse,* walked into the apartment without ceremony." This is the military representative of the government, General Campbell. The Prince offers to give himself up to save his friends. This recalls the half-hearted Jacobites to memories of honour, and they "would have seized or struck down Campbell, had it not been that he remained with his arms folded, and a look rather indicating impatience because they would not hear him than the least apprehension of violence at their hands.

At length he obtained a moment's silence. 'I do not, he said, 'know this gentleman (making a profound bow to the unfortunate Prince)—I do not wish to know him; it is a knowledge which would suit neither of us.' "

This is perhaps the finest passage in all Scott's works. The emotional effect of the contrast between the confused fear of the arrival of Campbell with irresistible military force and his actual solitary entry is very great. And I confess that the feeling excited in me is even stronger now than when I first read *Redgauntlet* twenty years ago. Baron Bradwardine had spoken long before in *Waverley* of the end of an old song, but his words were premature. Here is the very end; and it is an end as logical as it is surprising. General Campbell enforces from the distant but near world of everyday politics and eighteenth century common sense the same lesson that the angry quarrel between the Prince and Sir Richard Glendale had taught inwardly. They are not truly Jacobites any more. When he pretends not to know the Prince, and suggests that they have met together for bear-baiting or cock-fighting, he is, of course, speaking with the prudence of the practical politician, who wants no more fuss than is necessary. But he is also speaking a symbolic truth that goes home to the hearts of all of them except Redgauntlet himself. And the unwilling presence of Redgauntlet's kidnapped nephew, the head of his family, who does not even fancy himself to be a Jacobite, is appropriate too.

It remains that even Redgauntlet must be made to see that the end has come. A man whose courage cannot be quelled, and whose devotion is unlimited, must be made to admit defeat. This is achieved in the only way possible, by clemency. They are all, says Campbell, free to go. Nothing will be remembered against anyone. No one, except the Prince himself, need go into exile. " 'Is this real?' asks Redgauntlet, 'Can you mean this?' . . . 'then, gentlemen, the cause is lost for ever.' "

But how characteristic of Scott it is that he does not end quite here with the most moving climax he ever wrote. He shows us the squalid corpses of the only two men who shed blood in this affair, the traitor Cristal Nixon, and the strange, off-beat, dishonourable avenger Nanty Ewart. ('That sound broadsword cut', said Campbell, 'has saved us the shame of rewarding a traitor.') We see the ignominious but touching departure of the Prince and Redgauntlet alone, while the others wait a little ashamed on the shore and prepare to make their peace with a generous and paternal government. Only Redgauntlet and Campbell help the Prince on to the boat; a strange fellow-feeling develops between those who have throughout been true to their principles, though forced into alliance with waverers. The end of the book, and the end of the whole long Jacobite adventure can only be anti-climax.

At the end of Scott's last great novel we are aware that the man who had responded with so much feeling to the heroic has many unexpected modes of thinking and feeling. No simple formula will explain him. The rich variety of the traditions that formed him is matched by the complexity within.

Index

Abbot, The 42, 92
Antiquary, The 13, 40, 42-53, 80
Arnold, Matthew 32
Austen, Jane 13, 63, 65

Bagehot, Walter 133
Betrothed, The 94-97
Black Dwarf, The 13, 19
Blake, William 19, 61
Bride of Lammermoor, The 13, 42, 81-89
Browne, Sir Thomas 131
Browning, Robert 51, 156
Burns, Robert 25-6
Byron, Lord 14, 28, 33, 100

Carlyle, Thomas 70, 162
Castle Dangerous 86n
Castle of Otranto, The (Horace Walpole) 81, 91
Charles Edward, the Young Pretender 15, 107
Chronicles of the Canongate 18, 54
Clarissa Harlowe (Richardson) 63
Coleridge, S. T. 30, 57
Collins, Wilkie 185
Conrad, Joseph 127
Coriolanus (Shakespeare) 189
Count Robert of Paris 100
Covenanters 129-151
Critic, The (Sheridan) 32
Cromwell, Oliver 25

Davie, Donald 153n, 171
Dickens, Charles 63, 64, 100, 163, 167

Disraeli, Benjamin 64
Drumclog, battle of 65-70
Dryden, John 21, 23, 25

Egoist, The (Meredith) 64
Eliot, George 63, 148
Eliot, T. S. 32
Emma (Jane Austen) 63

Fair Maid of Perth, The 94
Fielding, Henry 185
Fortunes of Nigel, The 13
Froude, J. A. 162

George IV 13-16
Gibbon, Edmund 77-9, 100-1, 131-2, 145
Gray, Thomas 25
Great Expectations (Dickens) 164
Gulliver's Travels (Swift) 72
Guy Mannering 13, 31-41, 65, 154

Hall, Captain 23
Hardy, Thomas 156
Hawthorne, Nathaniel 84
Heart of Midlothian, The 13, 22, 42, 73, 80, 129, 171-192
Highland Widow, The 54-62, 90
History of America (Robertson) 24
Hume, David 21, 24-6, 49, 61, 129-132, 134-6, 148

Ivanhoe 13, 31, 81, 94, 97-100

Jacobites 13-16, 107-128, 152-170, 193-213

Johnson, Samuel 23, 25, 58, 61, 78, 79, 126
Journey to the Western Islands of Scotland (Johnson) 23, 78-9

Keats, John 30
Kenilworth 13, 94, 97
King Lear (Shakespeare) 102-3

Lady of the Lake, The 30
Leavis, F. R. 171
Legend of Montrose, A 13
Leopold of Saxe-Coburg, Prince 16
Little Dorrit (Dickens) 163
Lives of the Poets (Johnson) 79
Lockhart, J. G. 14-15
Lubbock, Percy 154
Lukacs, Georg 159n

Mackenzie, Henry 24-5
Marmion 31
Meadowbank, Lord 18
Middlemarch (Eliot) 148
Monastery, The 13, 73
Muir, Edwin 26-8

Nostromo (Conrad) 127

Old English Baron, The (Reeve) 102
Old Mortality 13, 21, 38, 59, 65-72, 80, 97, 104, 129-151

Peacock, T. L. 64
Peveril of the Peak 73-7, 97
Pirate, The 13, 22-3, 42, 48-51, 87-8
Pope, Alexander 61, 77-8

Porteous Riots 181

Quarterly Review, The 19
Quentin Durward 92-4, 101

Radcliffe, Ann 91
Redgauntlet 11-12, 16, 54, 80, 90, 104, 109, 127, 193-213
Reeve, Clara 102
Richardson, Samuel 25, 63, 65
Rob Roy 13, 16, 80, 87, 96, 127, 152-170
Robertson, William 21, 24-5, 61
Roman Pictures (Lubbock) 154
Romola (Eliot) 91
Rousseau, Jean-Jacques 61

St. Ronan's Well 13
Shaw, Bernard 43
Sheridan, R. B. 32

Talisman, The 92
Tom Jones (Fielding) 63
Two Drovers, The 21, 54, 58-60

Voltaire 61

Waverley 13, 15-16, 18, 70, 81, 87, 94, 104, 107-128, 153, 155-7, 165, 172
Woodstock 152
Woolf, Virginia 17, 26, 27
Wordsworth, William 19, 30-1, 47

Yonge, Charlotte 156
Young, G. M. 97